THE GOOD STUFF

COLUMNS ABOUT THE MAGIC OF SPORTS

THE GOOD STUFF

COLUMNS ABOUT
THE MAGIC
OF SPORTS

BY JOE POSNANSKI

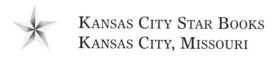
KANSAS CITY STAR BOOKS
KANSAS CITY, MISSOURI

These essays appeared first in *The Kansas City Star*.

Published by KANSAS CITY STAR BOOKS
1729 Grand Boulevard, Kansas City, Missouri 64108

First Edition

Library of Congress Control Number: 2001091263

ISBN 0-9709131-5-X

Editor: Monroe Dodd
Design: Jean Donaldson Dodd
Dust Jacket Front Photograph: Jim Barcus

Printed in the United States of America
by Walsworth Publishing Co., Inc.
Marceline, Missouri

To Mom and Dad

CONTENTS

I

II

III

IV

V

CONTENTS

VI

VII

VIII

PHOTOGRAPHS

Kansas City Star staff except where noted.

FOREWORD

People are nice. Every year, I hear from thousands of readers, and you would think that because I am a sports columnist spewing my stupid opinions that most of those would go along the lines of "You jerk," or, more precisely, "You big jerk." Of course, there are some of those.

But the vast, vast majority of letters are so nice — absurdly nice, preposterously nice, as if they were written by loving aunts or proud older brothers. They thank me — thank me? — for traveling the country, talking with the greatest athletes, writing columns. Why are they thanking me? I've got the best job on earth. You might remember the line from "Seinfeld"; Jerry was talking about his jobless and charmed neighbor Kramer. He said, "His life's a fantasy camp."

That's it exactly. My life's a fantasy camp.

"You know why I like you so much?" a reader said to me once, and before I could stop him he said, "It's because you love sports, and you're not ashamed of it."

See what I mean about readers being nice?

But maybe there is something to that. There is so much negativity out there. So much anger. So much "Fire-the-coach," and "Another-star-arrested," and "Ballplayer-chases-money-again." So much.

I write those things too sometimes. You can't get away. But most of the time, I don't write that. Most of the time I get to write

FOREWORD

the good stuff — about Charlie Brown and other heroes, baseball card gum and relief pitchers who write poetry and Buck O'Neil. And people thank me. Really, of course, they're not thanking me. They're thankful for the good stuff in sports. We're sports fans. We love the good stuff.

A few words about these columns: They are as they appeared in the newspaper, with all the flaws and rushed words of deadline writing. In a few cases, my editor, Monroe Dodd, did make small changes, but only for the sake of clarity.

Quick acknowledgements: I thank Monroe and Jean Dodd for putting this book together through all the headaches. My sports editor and friend Mike Fannin helped more than he knows. Four close friends — Richard Bush, Jim Banks, Michael MacCambridge and Mike Vaccaro — were there for me when it looked like we would never, ever come up with a title (Original title: "Dave Barry Writes Sports" was rejected for what now seem obvious copyright reasons). Thanks to my man, Dinn Mann, for bringing me to Kansas City, the place that has become home. And above all, thanks to Margo, who is not only my love and inspiration, but also a darned good character for my columns, even when she doesn't want to be.

Joe Posnanski
May 2001

LIKE A CHAMPION

All game long, I watched Will Shields. Couldn't take my eyes off the man. There he was, out of position, in bitter cold, in howling wind, in a meaningless game, performing in front of a half-empty stadium, and he played his heart out. He played from the soul.

Man, it was beautiful.

You can get all caught up in this crazy game, boo the quarterback, fire the coach, attack the general manager, all that, and if you're not careful you might miss something special. Something important.

Sunday afternoon, Will Shields started at left tackle for the first time since his high school days. And what was on the line, really? The Chiefs are not going to make the playoffs. Neither are the Carolina Panthers. The weather was lousy, the ball was as hard as Dan Snyder's heart, and the stadium was quieter than it has been since the last Wizards home game.

And there was right guard Will Shields playing left tackle for the first time in 13 years because John Tait got hurt. Do you know how hard it is to play left tackle in the NFL? You're protecting the quarterback against some of the meanest, fastest, most ferocious giants in all the world. This day, Shields battled Jay Williams, a 280-

pound former basketball player who just keeps coming all day long, like Joe Frazier.

Then, just for fun, Reggie White, the greatest defensive end to ever play the game, wandered over occasionally to face off against Shields.

"You're all alone out there at left tackle," Chiefs center Tim Grunhard said. "It's your own little world. One little mistake, and you're dead."

The Panthers sent a flurry of players at Shields, a whirlwind of moves, a barrage of hands and legs and elbows and helmets, all flying fast, furious. You block one player and two more appear in his place, you chase this guy and that guy sneaks behind you. It's like standing alone on the South Carolina coast and trying to block a hurricane.

And that's just what Will Shields did Sunday. He blocked a hurricane. No matter what the Panthers threw his way, he blocked it. Shields would say he felt uncomfortable. He felt bewildered. It didn't show. Jay Williams had one tackle. Nobody sacked Elvis Grbac. Shields was everywhere, stopping Williams, bumping White, knocking down a blitzing linebacker, then hopping back to Williams, like a square dancer bouncing from partner to partner.

"Will is the greatest athlete I've ever been around at the offensive-line position," Grbac said. "He's incredible."

"He's unbelievable," Chiefs coach Gunther Cunningham said.

"One of the best to ever play this game," Grunhard said.

Of course, you could write that story every single week: The incredible Will Shields. Most people will never understand the greatness of Shields until he's gone because he performs so quietly, so efficiently. He has gone to five straight Pro Bowls not so much for what he does, but for what he doesn't do. He doesn't jump offside. He doesn't hold. He doesn't miss blocks. He doesn't allow sacks. He doesn't complain.

Here's the greatest thing you can say about Shields, the greatest thing, really, you can say about an offensive lineman: You can go years and years without ever even thinking about the guy.

But there was something more remarkable about Shields' game on Sunday. Something different. Something that clutches the heart. I know a teacher who makes pitiful money, but she stays after school every single day because there's a child in her class who wants to become a better reader. I know a carpenter who will spend extra hours sealing the tiniest cracks, the ones the customer would never notice, because he believes in doing a job well.

I know a piano player who goes until the very last customer leaves because she loves to play music. I know a baseball scout who will drive two-lane roads all day if there's a chance he might see a good ballplayer. I know my father has worked hard every single day of his life, excepting Thanksgiving and Christmas, because of an old axiom — an honest day's work for an honest day's pay.

And Sunday, we watched Will Shields give an honest day's work. Who would have noticed if he had taken a play off here and there? The playoffs are gone. The Chiefs turned the ball over the first four times they had it. Empty seats filled the stadium. Heck, a lot of people around town want the Chiefs to lose so they can get a higher draft pick, so coaches will get fired, so season-ticket holders will give up their precious seats.

Who could have blamed Shields? Who would have even noticed?

But Shields just kept playing with every ounce of emotion he carries inside that giant body. Yes, he makes a lot of money, but it's not money that drives a man when his legs ache, when his arms feel like anvils, when the wind blows ice, when huge men are lunging at him. No, it's not money.

And it's not fame. Shields does not care about fame. He does so many good things for children around town, but he does it all quietly. He just wants to live a quiet life with his family.

And it's not cheers. You know that because there were precious few cheers Sunday at Arrowhead.

No, it's something else that spurs Shields, something about pride, something about loyalty, something about love. If you get the chance, take a minute today to think about Will Shields. Tell your children about him. Call the radio station about him. Sunday, with nothing at stake but a little pride and the hopes of a few thousand fans who have not yet given up faith, Shields played like a champion. Sure, it's just sports. But that's the stuff heroes are made of.

— **Dec. 11, 2000**

WATSON: A MOSAIC

There's a wonderful photograph of Tom Watson in 1975 at Carnoustie Golf Links in Scotland. He was just a kid then. The photograph was snapped years before he would stare down Jack Nicklaus and become the world's greatest golfer, the best golfer, in fact, of the last 25 years.

The photo was snapped long before Watson's putting stroke abandoned him, before sweet souls across America, so desperate to see Watson return to brilliance, sent him makeshift putters and homespun secrets they thought might make the ball roll a bit straighter.

In the photograph, Watson looks thrilled, like a child just about ready to hit the dessert tray at Sizzler. He wears a plaid knit cap, and long hair flows from underneath, and he smiles that gap-toothed smile and, yes, as writers would scribble mindlessly for two decades, he looks like Huck Finn.

"You always looked so at home over there," you tell him.

"You know, I really did not like playing over there," he says.

Then Watson — who has won five British Opens, more than any other American — tells you how he despised all those humps in the Scottish fairways and the way you had to roll the ball to the green and those pot bunkers, so deep you could hide the Portland Trail Blazers inside.

He disliked it all because often he would hit a good shot, a wonderful shot, and the ball would hit one of those mounds, kick behind a tree, into sand. Watson, above all, is a man of simple principles. If you hit a bad shot, in golf or in life, you should pay the penalty. Watson has hit his bad shots in both. He has always, in his own words, taken his medicine.

But Watson believes, just as deeply, that good shots should be rewarded.

"Then, I learned something," Watson says. "I learned that golf, like life, is not meant to be fair."

*   *   *

This is a story of little stories, of photographs and quotes and small tales. Maybe, put together, they will build a small mosaic of Kansas City's worldwide ambassador, Tom Watson, as he returns to Carnoustie for the British Open.

He tells so little of himself. Watson is the most private of public men. He has won eight major championships and was PGA Tour player of the year six times in eight years. He has never written an autobiography nor lent his life story to a ghost writer (there are at least 25 Tiger Woods biographies out there). He does no broadcasting, no autograph shows, no Barbara Walters-style interviews. He will talk elegantly for hours about his beloved Royals or the history of golf or the attributes of President Clinton.

Ask him a question about himself, though, and he might, if you're a friend, offer a little story.

*   *   *

Watson is 49 years old, almost 50, and he's back at Carnoustie, preparing for another British Open. He won his first Open at Carnoustie shockingly, without warning. He looked up at the scoreboard with one hole to play and realized, "Hey, if I birdie this, I can still win." He birdied 18.

The next day he found himself in an 18-hole playoff with Jack Newton, a hard-drinking, hard-smoking, hard-living Australian. They were a couple of 25-year-old kids who did not know any better. All day, they matched brilliance and clumsiness. Watson parred the last hole. Newton did not.

You ask Watson about the long, fun, painful and altogether wonderful journey he has trekked from Carnoustie then to Carnoustie now. He smiles.

"I just want to par No. 16 at Carnoustie," he says. "That's my only goal. I never parred that hole while I was there. Not once."

*   *   *

There's a wonderful photograph, the first one you see as you walk into the waiting room of Tom Watson's Westwood office. It's a photo from 1982, Pebble Beach, where Watson chipped in and beat Nicklaus at the U.S. Open.

But it is not a picture of the chip or of Watson celebrating or even of him accepting the U.S. Open trophy he had coveted all his life. Instead, it is a photograph of Nicklaus standing behind a lectern during the trophy presentation. Next to him is former President Gerald Ford.

Behind them, somewhat obscured and out of focus, is Tom Watson.

*   *   *

Over the years, many people have offered many dollars for Watson to re-enact the Pebble Beach chip. The chip has grown into legend. In one poll, golf fans voted it the most famous golf shot of all time, and why not? There was Watson in the rough on No. 17 on America's most famous public golf course. He was tied with Nicklaus, who was so certain that Watson would bogey the hole that he was accepting congratulations from friends.

"Get it close," said Watson's caddie, Bruce Edwards.

"I'm going to knock it in," Watson said back.

The ball went in, and Watson raced around the green. It's all golf lore now, as familiar as childhood fairy tales to golf fans across America. What isn't as well known is that, quite often, someone asks Watson's agent, Chuck Rubin, whether Watson would chip it again, you know, for the cameras, for a story, for television, for big money. Rubin shakes his head.

"Those people just don't know Tom Watson," he says. "He would never do that. He would never cheapen the shot. But that's the time we live in. Everyone wants to know how the magician does the trick."

Rubin shakes his head once more.

"People just don't want any magic in their lives anymore," he says.

*   *   *

Tom Watson on playing in bad weather: "I've seen other golfers give up. They don't want to play in the rain, in the cold, in the wind. It's too hard. But that's a part of golf. That's a part of life, too. You have to be tough. You have to hit the ball through the wind."

*   *   *

There's a wonderful photograph of Watson breaking through the crowd at Royal Birkdale in 1983, when he won his last British Open. He had hit a 2-iron, the best 2-iron of his life, right up on the green, and he thought it was good, but he could not see. Just as he hit the ball, the crowd closed around him like the sea crashing back in "The Ten Commandments."

Watson and his caddie, Alfie Fyles, bumped and pushed through the crowd. They could not see. They could only hear, and what they heard was this roar, this incredible roar, and now they knew the shot was good, very good, and they pushed a little harder, moved a little faster.

When Watson broke through, he saw the ball nestled up to the flagstick, and he raised his arms, as if he were signaling "Touchdown," and behind him fans screamed and wowed and tried to catch a peek of Watson. That's when the camera snapped. Little did he know this would more or less be it, that he would never again win a major championship, that within two years he would more or less stop winning golf tournaments altogether.

Even the greatest golfers — except Nicklaus — get such a short time on top of the world. Arnold Palmer got seven years. Ben Hogan, probably because of the bus accident that nearly killed him, only got six. Sam Snead's beautiful swing held up for decades, but he won his eight majors in seven years. Lee Trevino had seven years when he stood in the heavens with Nicklaus. Nick Faldo's passion burned hot for seven years.

Tom Watson would win some golf tournaments the next season, he would nearly win both the Masters and the British Open, but really, in so many ways, his seven-year reign ended after that 2-iron along the Lancashire Coast of England.

"I love that photograph," Watson says. "There's so much detail."

*   *   *

"What is your legacy?" a reporter asked this year at the Children's Mercy Golf Classic, a Watson charity event that has raised millions of dollars through the years to aid suffering children.

"I just hope," Watson said, "people remember me as a good guy."

*   *   *

Tom Watson is so beloved in Britain that he was recently made an honorary member of the Royal and Ancient Club. Numerous hotels there have rooms named for him. He is the honorary speaker for the Scottish Golf Writers virtually every year. They adore Watson in a way that even hometown people in Kansas City cannot fathom.

"Watching Watson in an Open," John Hopkins of *The Times* of London once wrote, "is like rounding a corner in Verona and coming upon Romeo and Juliet stealing a kiss."

*　　　*　　　*

Chuck Rubin is often asked why he and Tom Watson are still together. Rubin has been Watson's agent for more than a quarter-century. His walls are lined with putters people have sent Watson through the years.

Together, they have molded Watson's image as a man of substance, spurning cheap publicity stunts, always tying in with stable, refined companies like Polo, Cadillac and E.F. Hutton. They were a strong team. They were also brothers-in-law.

Two years ago, Watson and Linda Rubin divorced after 25 years of marriage. The divorce has been hard on the family, hard on the children, hard on Linda, hard on Tom. There's a lot of pain there.

Somehow, the partnership between Chuck Rubin and Tom Watson endures.

"I've known Tom for 35 years," Rubin says. "It's hard, emotionally, because we go to family functions, and Tom's not there anymore. It's hard because we're dealing with family, with my brother and sister, with my niece and nephew. Tom and I don't talk about it. I don't ask. He doesn't ask.

"You see, I don't judge Tom."

*　　　*　　　*

Gary Player on Tom Watson: "Nobody practiced like Tom when

he was young. It wasn't just the time he put in. It was the intensity. Every swing was to win the Open."

*   *   *

By September, Tom Watson expects to be in the best shape of his life. He's going on the Senior PGA Tour. He will be ready for that.

"I think Tom will dominate the senior tour," Nicklaus says. "Of course he will."

Watson would never say that. But, in his heart, he must believe it. Watson has spent the last 15 years scrambling with the kids, missing putts, missing fairways, missing cuts. Parts of his game would be breathtaking — as recently as two years ago, he was still considered the purest ball striker on the tour — but he would miss putts or hook his drives or something.

He was growing old.

Golf, though, gives athletes the rarest gift. It gives golfers a chance to be young again. So, Watson goes on tour once more, this time with the same old men he thrashed so long ago. He will again get to face Hale Irwin and Ray Floyd and Nicklaus. He will again get to be in contention every week.

"I'm excited," he says. "But I still think I can play with the kids."

*   *   *

Tom Watson tells you that, five times in his life, he felt absolutely certain that he would win a golf tournament before it ever started. A different feeling came over him, a jolt of confidence, a sense of calm. He just knew the tournament would be his and his alone.

"What were those tournaments?" you ask him.

"I'm not going to tell you," he says. "All I will tell you is I won four of them."

*   *   *

Tom Watson has helped write and rewrite *The Rules of Golf*. He has released *The Illustrated Rules of Golf*. He loves rules. He loves justice. He is sickened by the rampant injustice of other sports, such as baseball, in which everyone says the ball is wound too tight but nobody will actually do anything about it.

"You've got to have rules," he says. "That's the problem with the world today. There are no rules."

*   *   *

There's a wonderful photograph, Watson's favorite in fact, from Turnberry in '77. That was when Watson and Nicklaus played their great duel in the sun. Watson led Nicklaus by 1 at the British Open going into the 18th hole. The next closest golfer was Hubert Green, 11 shots back. "I won the golf tournament," Green would say later. "I don't know what game those other two guys were playing."

The crowd was crazy, the golf course beautiful, the sense of history as thick as a Scottish fog. Nicklaus was in the rough, in trouble, and Watson realized he could grab the world right there. He pulled out a 7-iron and hit the ball. A Japanese photographer snapped the camera just then.

"It's all there," Watson says. "You can see the ball. You can see the flag. You can see the fans. I'm wearing those checkered pants.

You can see those. It's all there, everything. That was the moment. That was the moment."

The golf ball landed 2 feet from the flag. Watson beat Nicklaus.

*　　　*　　　*

Tom Watson on the tears he cried at Colonial last year, when he won that tournament and was, for a week at least, the best in the world once more: "That was something. I was young again."

*　　　*　　　*

Why Tom Watson?

Chuck Rubin: "I don't really have an answer for that. I just know he worked hard."

Ben Crenshaw: "He was tougher than everyone else. When he needed a great shot, he hit a great shot."

Davis Love III: "He was the best putter in the world. He never left a putt short. I remember watching him play with my father, and Dad would say, 'Watch the way he attacks the hole.' Nobody attacked the hole like Tom Watson."

Nicklaus: "He always knew exactly where he was going."

Caddie Bruce Edwards: "He's taught me so much about golf and life. I don't know anyone who thinks things through so well. Any situation, Tom knows exactly what to do."

Watson: "I don't know. When I was young, I could really putt, and that's how you win. But I think somewhere in there I learned how to stay composed. People always say that I did not let a bad shot bother me, but I think the opposite is just as true. I tried not to let the good shots pump me up too much. Stay even-keeled. I think that was the key."

*   *   *

Tom Watson really disliked playing in Britain, even after Carnoustie in '75, even after Turnberry in '77. Then, one day, simply, he decided to love it. That's all. He just decided it was silly to hate a kind of golf because of a few bumps and a few unlucky breaks.

"You know what I did?" he asks, and he tells a story. One day in 1979, before the British Open, he thought for a long time about golf. He thought about when he was growing up in Kansas City, how he used to play with his father, Ray, and all of Ray's buddies at Kansas City Country Club. They called him Flytrap Finnegan then, after a talkative caddie in the comics. It was an inside joke. Tom Watson never said a word on the golf course.

He thought about how much he loved playing golf, and that was long before the championships, long before he ever dreamed of being the best in the world. He played in the rain and the wind and the snow, not for money, not for fame, not for trophies, not for love.

He just loved rolling the ball up to the flag.

"And you know what British golf is?" Watson asks, as he prepares for the punch line. "It's just rolling the ball up to the flag. It's just the same kind of golf I grew up with. It's just rolling the ball up to the flag."

— **July 12, 1999**

YOU PUNCH THE GUY,
HE PUNCHES YOU BACK

S pend two minutes with Blades defenseman Dean Ewen on Wednesday night, and you could call it quality time. We share the penalty box late in the first period. It is definitely a bonding thing. Ewen glares straight ahead. I glare straight ahead. Wendy, our photographer, takes pictures.

"Who was that photographer?" Ewen asks the next time he stops by.

"She's with the paper."

"I was about to cross-check her right in the head," he says. "She was flashing that flash in my eyes. I wasn't in a good mood."

Dean Ewen is 6 feet 2. He weighs 220 pounds. He has spent more than 11 hours in penalty boxes since becoming a hockey professional. He smiles just a little bit as if he just might be joking about that head-checking thing.

"I'm in a better mood now," he says.

Five minutes later, Ewen beats up two guys on the Manitoba Moose, and then he goes after a third.

Nothing else in sports touches the penalty box. In football, you do something terribly wrong, they throw yellow flags at you. In baseball, they ask you to leave the premises. In pro basketball, they blow whistles and point. In college basketball, they make you the University of Cincinnati coach.

But in hockey, they shove you in here, the box, where you serve time. No trial. No jury. No appeals. No Johnnie Cochran. The referee points, and you are sentenced, two to five minutes, sometimes longer. Not that the penalty box is so bad. It's carpeted. It has big windows. There is cold water available. Heck, it's better than half the apartments in New York. And you can always talk to Dave, the gatekeeper, who has been doing this for years.

"You want some cold water?" Dave asks.

"NO!" Jason Cirone screams.

"OK," Dave says.

No, there isn't exactly sterling conversation in the penalty box Wednesday night, my night in the penalty box. The Blades stink up the joint. They lose 7-2, and even die-hard Blades fans — you've got to figure most of the 3,157 in the crowd are die-hards — boo like this is the Steve Bono reunion tour.

Sure, it's a lousy night on the ice, but there is plenty of action in the box. At one point, I am joined by three Blades players, all in there for some horrible crime. You may wonder what it's like to be stuffed into a box with three huge, angry, sweaty hockey players. Probably not. I never did before.

Truth is, it's not very exciting. You might think they would be asking each other "Hey, whatcha in for?" You might think they would be bragging about their exploits ("Sure, I slashed him. Slashed him right in the leg. And I'd do it again") or mocking the inmate who was called for delay of game ("Ooh, Mr. Slowpoke") or at least threatening the linesmen.

Really, they spit. That's about it. They spit, and they curse with cool Canadian accents, and then they spit some more. Cirone is probably the best spitter on the team. Hey, he's a hockey veteran. He can spit water so far, the referee calls icing.

Some guys are friendly in the penalty box. It depends. Take Claudio Scremin. He interferes with somebody — hardly the most vicious of penalties — and so he wanders in the box, poses for pictures, talks a bit. "I didn't do it," he says. That's the way it usually goes with those guys who just interfere or hook or hold or some other minor offense.

Players do tend to be edgy in the box after fights, though. It's quite simple, really. They wish they were still fighting. There is nothing in hockey quite like the thrill of the fight. The crowd is loud — even the prettiest overtime goal will not excite people like a fight — everybody's watching, and there's no subtlety. You punch the guy. He punches you back. Nobody calls a two-line pass during fights.

So, Darin Kimble skates into the box after his fight, which he won easily, and this seems a good time to explore the reasons behind hockey fights. In no other team sport is fighting such a big part of the game. What's the sociological reason? Where does this aggression originate?

"Uh," I begin.

Kimble doesn't seem in the best talking mood. In fact, he's now shoving me to the side. And he's still shoving. And now, I'm hanging off the bench, squashed against the Plexiglas. Three women on the other side laugh at me. A guy raises up his drink to me.

"Uh," I start again.

Kimble looks at me. He's 6 feet 2. He weighs 215 pounds. He has spent more than 29 hours in penalty boxes, from Manitoba to Las Vegas to Kansas City. He does not look as if he will buy me a beer. He looks as if he will cross-check me right in the head.

"Never mind," I say.

He nods, spits and returns to the game.

— **Oct. 30, 1997**

T H E W O R L D T U R N E D U P S I D E D O W N

The trouble with being a walking, breathing, living hero is that you never get a day off. There are no weekends. No coffee breaks. No vacations. Every morning, Steve Palermo wakes up, swings around to get out of bed, and then he reaches for his cane. The pain awakens. It bursts through his legs. The cheers have quieted for him. The applause has faded. The flowers have stopped coming. But every morning, without exception, the same white-hot pain wakes up with Palermo.

"I've never liked all that hero talk anyway," Palermo says.

*　　　*　　　*

Everywhere Steve Palermo goes, they ask him the same question: Would you do it again? It's such a human question. They don't often ask "Why did you do it?" or "Were you afraid?" or "What were you thinking on that night?" Those questions don't quite get to the point.

No. It's simply this: Would you do it again?

On July 6, 1991, Palermo was in Campisi's Egyptian Restaurant, which is actually a little Italian place in Dallas, run by a good friend, Corky Campisi. Corky was there, of course, and so were other guys. They were all laughing. This was Dallas, but it could have been Chicago or Detroit or Boston or any other major-league town. It was just another night for Palermo, a major-league umpire. This was his life. He slept late, umpired games in the evenings, ate at the best restaurants, drank with good friends.

"Someday Stevie," his mother, Angela, would say all the time, "you'll get a real job, right?"

"Yeah, Ma," Stevie said. "Someday."

He felt relaxed. It had been an easy umpiring night for Palermo. A kid named Kevin Brown had pitched well. There were no close plays at third base. He laughed easily. He did love this life.

Then Jimmy Upton, the bartender, yelled suddenly: "Two waitresses are getting mugged across the street."

Palermo and five guys rushed into the street.

They did not think about it.

They chased after the three muggers.

Two took off in a car. Some of the guys went after the car. Palermo and a friend chased the man on foot. They pinned him to the ground. Then, the car returned.

Tires squealed. Bullets flew.

The last bullet hit Palermo in the back. His legs, instantly, went numb.

"Would you do it again?" they ask Steve Palermo, from Boston to San Francisco, children and adults, men and women, all races, all faiths. The real question behind that, of course, is, "If I were in that restaurant, that night, would I have done the same thing?"

*   *   *

Steve Palermo did love umpiring. He was born to umpire. Even as a kid in Oxford, in the heart of Massachusetts, in the guts of Red Sox country, he loved baseball more than the Red Sox. He cared more about the game than winning and losing. His dad, Vincent, cherished the Red Sox. But Stevie watched the games from a distance. He had the umpire's soul.

Palermo was 20 when an old family friend and a scout caught

him umpiring a local all-star game. Six years later, Palermo was in Toronto in April, umpiring the first Blue Jays game ever. It was freezing. The Zamboni was out clearing snow off the field.

What a ride. He brought his Pops to Fenway. Vinny Palermo wandered around with his mouth open. He could not even talk. Jim Rice, the great Boston slugger, came up the stairs with a tray of coffee for them both. "Jimmy, I don't care how much coffee you bring us," Steve said, "you're still not getting that pitch on the outside corner."

New York Yankees manager Billy Martin walked by.

"Stevie," Vincent said. "Do you know who that is?"

"Know who he is?" Stevie said. "Dad, I yelled at him last night."

What a ride. Stevie called the Bucky Dent home run fair, and he was behind the plate when Dave Righetti threw his Independence Day no-hitter, and he joked with fans in the stands, and he called beautiful balls and strikes, and he made good friends in every big city in the country. He was at a Checkers Restaurant in Kansas City when he first saw Debbie Aaron. She was fresh out of college. He asked her out. She said no. He asked again.

"Who you going out with?" Steve Aaron asked his sister the next day.

"An umpire," Debbie said.

"I hope it's not that second-base umpire who blew two calls," he said.

Debbie went to dinner with Palermo, who was indeed that second-base umpire. She married him six years later. She married him five months before Steve went into Campisi's Egyptian for a little dinner and laughter with good friends after a Rangers game on a Saturday night.

*   *   *

Steve Palermo was a national phenomenon for a while. After the shooting, the ambulance took him to Parkland Memorial Hospital, the same hospital where John Kennedy was taken after he was shot. Within days there were three rooms jammed with flowers for Palermo. The phone would not stop ringing. Letters poured in. Ronald Reagan wrote. Nolan Ryan called. Ballplayers loitered in the waiting room. Millions prayed.

On a television screen, an ESPN announcer said that Palermo would almost certainly never walk again, the same thing doctors were telling Steve.

"You watch!" he screamed at the television screen. "You watch!"

Every day, Palermo fought to walk. No words can describe the agony of his journey. He has tried to explain the pain that would just buzz and burn through him, suddenly, as if he were being shocked. He has tried to explain the horror of fighting through it all, hour after hour, day after day, and then seeing so little progress that all he could do was sit in his bed and cry softly, so no one could hear. He has tried to explain for years.

"Inch by inch, life's a cinch," Debbie reminded him day after day. It became their mantra. More than that. They repeated the phrase so often, it was their life preserver, the one thing they could say when the pain was unbearable, when hope faded, when there was nothing else to say.

Months passed. Years. But Palermo did start to walk, first with crutches, then with canes, then finally with just one cane. America rejoiced. *Sports Illustrated* put his photo on the cover. George Will wrote about him. *The New York Times* had almost daily updates on him. Palermo threw out the first pitch of the World Series. "America's Most Wanted," came by to talk, as did "Entertainment

Tonight." "20/20" brought out its crew to tell his story, though the director seemed more interested in moving furniture around the Palermos' Overland Park house to make their shots look better.

"It was like the Mayflower moving people had come in," he says. "Debbie was furious."

For America, though, the story kind of ended there. Palermo said he would walk. He did walk. There's your Hollywood ending. Cue the sweeping music. Run the credits. Fade to black.

Only Steve Palermo's life kept going.

"The pain," he says softly, "never goes away."

*   *   *

He speaks in different towns now. Motivational stuff. He does some speaking for Fortis Benefits Insurance too. Then, he does some work for baseball. A few years ago, he came up with six easy and inspired ways to quicken the game's pace. They have not been implemented yet, of course. You might not know this, but some of the people who run baseball are not very smart.

Palermo and his family also raise money for the National Paralysis Foundation. They are not looking to help people deal with their paralysis. They want them all to walk again. Tonight, an old friend, Bob Costas, will come into town for his annual "Later With Bob Costas" dinner, to raise some money for spinal-cord research.

"You have a chance now to reach more people than you ever did as an umpire," Debbie tells Steve. Other friends tell him the same thing. Steve Palermo nods. He knows they are right. He counts his friends. He counts his blessings. He keeps speaking and working and raising money. "The Lord giveth," he says, "and the Lord taketh away."

Sometimes it's too hard, though. There are dark nights. There are moments of despair. There are no days off for a hero. Every morning the pain shoots through him. The cane is always there by his bed. The memories linger like cigar smoke. He was an umpire. He was a good umpire. He was living the life.

"Would you do it again?" they ask him over and over.

"It's the wrong question," Palermo says. He is quiet for a long while.

"Let me tell you something," he says finally. "I would do it again. You know why? Two reasons. One, if my wife was in that situation, I would hope four or five guys would come to her defense. I have to believe that. I want to believe that.

"Two, if I say no, I wouldn't do it again, then what does that mean? It means I made a mistake, right? I can't admit it was a mistake. I just can't admit that."

He pauses again. His phone rings. He does not pick up.

"I went to help people in trouble," he says. "How can that be a mistake?"

*   *   *

On a winter afternoon, Steve Palermo went golfing. He does love golfing. He gave it up for a long time because the pain was too great, but he's back again. He's back. And the sun was out that day.

"The world's turned upside down," he says. "It's warm in January. And I'm playing golf again. Who would ever have thought that?"

He shot 93, but it might have been better. One shot landed in an awkward place in a sand trap, and no matter how he tried, there was no way for Palermo to get to the ball. He took a penalty stroke. For a moment, he thought about how, before all this, he would have just walked up to the ball, knocked it on the green. The moment passed. Steve Palermo played through.

— **Jan. 14, 2000**

DiMaggio: Perfection

He was 84 years old and lived a life beyond the storybooks, a life of baseball and love and cheers that never hushed. Almost 50 years have drifted away since he played his last baseball game in 1951, but his fame never faded, his brilliance never dulled. In 1969, during baseball's centennial, he was declared the greatest living ballplayer. For the rest of his life, Joe DiMaggio would be introduced that way.

DiMaggio transcended sports, of course. He married Marilyn Monroe and, until his death early Monday, made certain that fresh roses adorned her grave. Ernest Hemingway wrote about him. Robert Frost admired him. Ronald Reagan adored him. Edward Mills Purcell, a Nobel physicist, would spend hours with his computer studying DiMaggio. A hit song of 1941 was called "Joltin' Joe DiMaggio."

Twenty-five years later, Paul Simon wrote the song lyrics that would forever be associated with him, lyrics DiMaggio never particularly liked: "Where have you gone, Joe DiMaggio? A nation turns its lonely eyes to you."

A song in the musical "South Pacific" compares a woman's skin to the tenderness of DiMaggio's glove.

He was known for his elegance. He said little. He showed no

emotion on the field. He made everything look easy. His old teammate, Yogi Berra, remembers that DiMaggio never dived for a baseball. His most famous achievement, appropriately, was not one moment, not one of his long home runs or a single great catch. Instead, it evolved over a two-month stretch in 1941 in the perilous time before America went to war. DiMaggio got hits in 56 consecutive games, a record never since approached. Every day, the nation stopped and closed in around the radio to hear whether Joltin' Joe had picked up another base hit.

But if DiMaggio was famous when he played, he became a folk hero in the years afterward, as sports moved into the realm of television and big business. He came to represent a lost grace in sports, a shriveling of the notion of athlete as American hero. Red Smith, considered by many the greatest sportswriter of all, ended the last column he ever wrote eerily. "I told myself not to worry," he wrote. "Some day there would be another Joe DiMaggio."

Red Smith wrote that 17 years ago. No Joe DiMaggio has ascended.

*   *   *

A strange thing happened Monday. All of these ballplayers across America turned poetic. All of these wonderful men who had spent so much of their lives swearing and spitting, reminiscing and telling dirty jokes, all of them spoke in hushed tones, reaching for the most lyrical and reverential words that they could find inside.

"If you said to God, 'Create someone who was what a baseball player should be,' God would have created Joe DiMaggio," Tommy Lasorda would say.

"I stopped and shook his hand," Hall of Famer Al Kaline said. "It was like meeting God."

"God's probably thrilled to meet Joe DiMaggio," Yogi Berra said.

Yes, God's name came up often, and maybe that's because people never seemed to have big enough words to describe DiMaggio. He was, at various times in his life, Joltin' Joe and the Yankee Clipper and the Great DiMaggio and Mister Coffee and the greatest living ballplayer, and none summed him up.

As a baseball player, he had to be seen to be appreciated. His statistics are not particularly overwhelming, and while much of that had to do with time (he missed three prime years because of World War II) and place (he played at cavernous Yankee Stadium), truth is, much of his splendid reputation also came from time (he played for some of the great teams in baseball history) and place (he played in New York when it was truly the center of the baseball world).

Still, the people who saw him play every day say that he was perfection, surely the greatest overall player who ever lived. He hardly ever swung and missed; in one entire season he struck out just 13 times. He never made great catches, but instead made every catch and made them all look easy. He could run and throw, hit and field, it was said he simply never made mistakes, and in his 13 seasons he propelled the Yankees to 10 World Series.

"He just did it every day," Berra said. "Some guys were great for 10 games or 20 games, but he was great all the time."

DiMaggio used to say that he had to be great every day. "There is always some kid who may be seeing me for the first time," he used to say. "Or the last time."

He took that very seriously. DiMaggio guarded his legend. Even when he was playing, he seemed to understand that people needed more from him, and so he said little, he dressed well, he did nothing that would steal from his splendor. He also withdrew from people. Some said he was shy, others thought him aloof, but he never changed. He despised the spotlight. He often called Marilyn Monroe the love of his life, but the attention heaped on them contributed to a divorce after only a year. A month ago, when he emerged from a well-publicized coma, he told the doctor to quit leaking his condition to the media.

"I don't have anything against sportswriters," he said a couple of years ago at Yankee Stadium. "I just wish they would quit writing about me."

*   *   *

This, of course, seems a time for deference, because Joe DiMaggio died, and he might have been the greatest baseball player of all time; surely he was the most revered and treasured athlete in American history.

But then, he was worshipped most of his life, so much so that it embarrassed him. His autograph shows were simply processions of admirers; people who gushed praise or were overwhelmed because for them, like Al Kaline, it was like meeting God. It was hard being a living folk hero, and once DiMaggio stopped a man in the middle of a particularly intense tribute and said, simply, "Look, I'm just a man. It's nice to meet you, too."

He had been immortalized by Hemingway. He had been on the cover of *Life*.

He met every president of his generation. He had heard all the cheers. He lived a good, good life. There are few words left to write about him.

A New York concierge once offered beautiful advice. He said: "If you're in an Italian restaurant anywhere in America, and you don't see a picture of Joe DiMaggio on the wall, walk out."

And over the years, one finds that, indeed, there almost always is better pasta in restaurants where Joe DiMaggio's photo is on the wall. Hard to say why. Then, DiMaggio always was a mystery.

— **March 9, 1999**

BEING TIGER WOODS' BALL

AUGUSTA, Ga. — From up here, you can see heaven. You can see shopping centers beyond the magnolias. You can see Paul Stankowski's shirt, which is louder than a Metallica concert. You can see Ike's tree and Rae's Creek and Amen Corner and the cars that rush by on Washington Road and a million people.

The people all scream advice.

"Bite," they yell.

"Big kick," they yell.

"Go left," they yell.

You wish they would shut up. You don't need any advice.

You are Tiger Woods' golf ball.

You don't need any help.

You are a handsome golf ball. Dimples. Hard body. You are a lucky golf ball. You don't get hit much. You don't have to take any baths. You are a good golf ball. You stay out of trouble. You don't hit people.

You saw Colin Montgomerie's ball hit people on Saturday.

Bad ball.

You are the best ball. You will win the Masters today. You will win by many, many shots. Nobody can stop that. Your boss, Tiger

Woods, is the greatest golfer in the world. He has played better than anyone ever this past week. He has hit you nine fewer times than any other golf ball. That's a lot. "Too far," you heard Costantino Rocca's ball say. His ball is the closest one.

You spoke to Tom Watson's ball, and according to her, Watson said: "I just want to play my best golf and try for second place."

All other golf balls play for second place.

It will be this way for the next 20 years.

You feel blessed. You sort of lucked into this gig. You were just a golf ball, one of millions, only you stretched out for Tiger Woods' hand when the Masters began. Kids screamed for you. They wanted Tiger to throw you away. Tiger, bless his heart, held on tight.

Then, heaven. Tiger makes you spin and pirouette and step back, like James Brown. He cuts you, fades you, hooks you, tickles you, smashes you. It is like dancing. On the 11th hole Saturday, he hit you into a gallery of people. You avoided the danger spots, found a nice soft place to land, and then he lifted you, higher and higher, and you rolled up to the hole. He hit you in, took you out, showed you to the crowd. Birdie, people said breathlessly.

The crowd cheered.

You bowed.

You flew over the green on No. 2, a treacherous thing, but then Tiger massaged you close to the hole and putted you in. On No. 5, you rolled 15 feet, veered slightly to the left, dropped softly into the hole. You flew over the water at Hole No. 12. You curled back toward the hole at No. 18.

Those cheers made the ground shake at 18.

Then, there are tough times, too, like at No. 13, when you whacked into a tree. That hurt. Then, Tiger sent you over the green, he had to chip you back, and then he hit you the wrong way on the putt. Groans carried over the water. Tiger winced. Man, that hurt. That's such an easy hole. You and Tiger usually breeze through that hole.

Sure, the other golf balls are jealous, but you know this is hard work. Sometimes, you would like a vacation. You soar over water and see other golf balls who scuba dive. You soar over sand, where your friends tan in the sun. You wonder what it would be like to lounge around, stretch in the high grass, maybe go camping in the woods.

You can't stop, though. You have a job to do.

"Go out and kick some butt," Woods' dad, Earl, told you and Tiger this morning. He says that every day. Yeah, it's tough, every day, you have to go out and kick some butt. No time to rest.

But, it will be worth it today. You will see more of heaven. You will fly higher than all the others, roll farther than any of them. And you will fly around Augusta one more time, you will see the golf course where Hogan's golf balls hit flagsticks, where Nicklaus' plopped in cups, where Palmer's heard cheers never heard before.

Your cheers will roar even louder today.

And, when it ends, Tiger Woods will get his green jacket, and you will go to some museum, and the game of golf forever will be changed. Oh yeah, Sunday will be a ball.

— **April 13, 1997**

THE CLOCK TICKS AWAY

Seconds pour away. Agony. Elvis Grbac screams to his teammates. They scream back. The crowd screams louder. Static rushes through Grbac's helmet. It is fourth down. Two yards to go. Seconds pour away.

"What's the play?" receiver Lake Dawson yells.

"We need a play," offensive lineman Dave Szott yells.

"He can't hear the play," offensive coordinator Paul Hackett yells.

Seconds pour away. Torture. Run? Pass? There are 44 seconds, no, 38 seconds, no, 37 seconds. Run? Pass? The Chiefs need the first down. The Chiefs need the touchdown. The Chiefs have no timeouts. Denver leads by four. Grbac can't hear anything. He is supposed to hear the play through speakers in his helmet. He is supposed to hear the soothing voice of coach Mike McCarthy. Static roars instead. "The NFL should have helmets that work," Grbac thinks. He is angry.

Seconds pour away.

Panic creeps into the crowd. Dread creeps into the stomachs of the fans. Something is not right. The clock ticks. Somebody do something. The fans yell. Teammates yell. Grbac needs to call a play. He needs to set up his offensive line. Seconds pour away. Static roars in his ears. "Sometimes a quarterback has to just make a call," Grbac realizes.

His teammates gather. Grbac calls to them. Thirty-three seconds. Thirty-two. In the booth above, Paul Hackett calls his play, a short pass, a shot at a quick first down, but he knows the play will never reach Grbac. He knows it will never be run. "It kills me," he would say. "Because that's my job. I call plays."

Instead, Grbac calls his own play. Some of his teammates hear it. Some cannot. Grbac waves to the crowd. He flaps his arms up and down. A bird. He begs them to be still. They cannot. Seconds pour away. The fans see the whole season crashing. The Chiefs were 13-3. The season was magic. The Chiefs mean so much here. There are 28 seconds, now 27, now 26. Somebody do something.

Agony. The Chiefs have no timeouts. They lost one of those in the red zone early in the second half. "We have to be sure there," Grbac would explain. They lost another because the play clock ran down midway through the third quarter. "We can't afford that," coach Marty Schottenheimer would explain.

Now the clock rushes wildly, out of control. One play earlier, tight end Ted Popson caught a pass. He could have run out of bounds. He could have stopped the clock. He could have stopped the madness.

"We talk about it all year, every day," Hackett would say. "You've got to be smart there."

Popson turned upfield. He tried to make a big play. He was tackled.

Seconds pour away.

"Listen to me, listen to me," Grbac screams to his teammates. He has a play. It is a bold play. Sometime in September, he and receiver Andre Rison connected on a bold play. Beat Oakland. Got this magic season rolling. Grbac wants bold again. He calls bold. It's a mistake.

"Let's do it," Lake Dawson says.

"Make it happen," someone yells.

"Right now," Grbac says.

Seconds pour away. Twenty-five seconds. Twenty-four. Stomachs twist. It feels as if the Chiefs have been talking for an hour. The fans are frenzied. Schottenheimer jumps up and down.

Derrick Thomas looks away. Teammates yell at Grbac.

"They were scurrying, they were hurried, they were rattled," Broncos linebacker Bill Romanowski would say.

Grbac screams the last instructions. Hackett sits in the booth, helpless, a fan. The Broncos jump around. They will blitz. They might fake the blitz. The Chiefs' players still are not set. Now, 23 seconds … 22 seconds … 21 seconds … 20.

A whole season for this one play.

Grbac takes the snap. He drops back. "Get the first down," Schottenheimer screams. The crowd drowns him. Grbac is not looking for the first down. Rison, heroic all day, runs a short route. Grbac is not looking his way. Popson, so desperate to atone, runs a short route. Grbac's eyes go elsewhere.

He looks for Lake Dawson, down the field, the end zone, the knife to the heart. He wants it now. He throws the ball left, into double coverage, into the end zone, hoping, believing. "Lake has made so many big plays, jumping over defenders," Grbac would say.

The sound in Arrowhead Stadium reaches its crescendo, a blur of noise, a rush of cheers and stomps and shrieks and wishes, whirling, reeling and then, suddenly, nothing.

The clock stops.

The ball never got to Lake Dawson. The Broncos run on the field. Twelve seconds remain.

And it hurts. The players ache. Schottenheimer wipes tears away. Grbac wipes tears away. Is there anything worse than this? All the fans sit in silence, air gone from their bodies. They stare out. The Broncos run their last play, a John Elway kneel, and the clock begins again, seconds pouring away, agony, torture, and there's no way to stop it.

— **Jan. 5, 1998**

IT WAS PURE LOVE, THAT'S ALL

STILLWATER, Okla. — Terrence Crawford decided to dunk. You're not really supposed to dunk the basketball during pre-game warmups. You're supposed to maintain your energy, save your fire, hold back the storm. Crawford, an Oklahoma State freshman, turned 19 Sunday. He had not played in 10 days. He could not wait any longer. He dunked the basketball before the Cowboys faced Missouri on Monday night.

And Andre Williams dunked.

And Fredrik Jonzen dunked.

And Jack Marlow dunked.

And that's when the people in Gallagher-Iba Arena began to really scream. For 10 days, they couldn't scream. They could only sob softly and whisper and hug and pray. Ten funerals scattered across cold Oklahoma days. Every hour, every minute, there was another reminder of that Oklahoma State plane going down, the shrieks, the crash, wives widowed in an instant, fathers and mothers losing sons.

"I had him for 31 years," Bill Hancock said of his son, Will, Monday morning, during the last of the memorial services.

"He was ... such ... a gift to me," Bill continued, and his voice broke, and he cried, and all of us in the church cried, and it was the most courageous and beautiful speech I've ever heard a man give. It was pure love, that's all. It was the sound of a heart breaking.

And that's the only sound you heard in Stillwater these last days. People kept sending flowers. Roses, tulips, violets and wildflowers swamped Gallagher-Iba and still more arrived. Oklahoma fans wept with Oklahoma State fans. Children kept writing poems. Radio callers kept sobbing. On every marquee, in front of every church and restaurant and dry cleaners, there was another phrase of love for the 10 men who died in the crash.

"We will remember you always."

"There are 10 Cowboys in heaven."

"Heroes are never forgotten."

The 10 days were so draining, exhausting and painful. It felt like a year. Nobody knew what it would be like when Missouri and Oklahoma State played basketball, the first game back. Nobody knew.

What happened was, the students stormed into the arena at 5:30 p.m. and rushed around to get the best seats, like students always do. Fans made silly faces into the television cameras for the simple reason that the cameras were on. A male cheerleader lifted a female cheerleader with one hand, as if to say, "Look people, I am a very strong man."

The band played "Oklahoma!," very loud. A woman with her face painted orange danced. A tiny ballboy dribbled a basketball between his legs.

How to react? Laugh? Cry? Go home? You just never know with sports. Much of the time, the games seem so important. They make our stomachs hurt, our throats burn, they leave us breathless. Then real tragedy creeps in — mothers' tears, strong voices silenced, best friends lost — and we realize that these games are so insignificant.

And it all felt so pointless Monday. But then, Terrence Crawford dunked in a pre-game warmup. Why? Because he could. And a teammate followed with a dunk, and another, and another, and the screams grew louder, and another dunk, and louder, and another dunk, and louder, and another dunk.

And all of a sudden, maybe it made just a little sense.

Life does go on. Life has to go on.

Oklahoma State and Missouri played a game filled with such passion, such fury, such love. It wasn't pretty basketball. There were a thousand missed shots and a million hard fouls and stomping coaches and players landing hard on the court.

But it was basketball played with joy. Crazy joy. These were kids playing harder than they ever thought possible, diving after basketballs, banging into each other, flying toward the basket, and all the while the sound in the arena kept swelling and surging until you could feel the sound rattling your spine.

And, in the second half, when Crawford stole the basketball, he saw nothing but the rim in front of him. He rose. He dunked for real. Oklahoma State led! The floor shook. Maurice Baker made back-to-back three-pointers. Oklahoma State led big! Hands waved wildly. Missouri's last chance to win was stolen by Melvin Sanders. Oklahoma State won!

People stood and screamed for a long, long, long time after that, amazed perhaps by their own sound. Players hugged. And, Eddie Sutton, the old Oklahoma State coach, allowed a tear or two to slip down his cheek.

"I don't think that I am the only one," Sutton said, "who shed a tear."

Of course, it does not make the pain go away. Sports can't do that. Ten people died. Friends. Sons. Fathers. Husbands. Hearts are broken, and no game can put those pieces together.

But maybe here's what sports can teach: When Quin Snyder was preparing his Missouri players to play this eerie game, he told them that sports are trivial and a basketball game has nothing to do with that bigger thing called life.

Then he told them this: "Play hard every play. That's how you can pay tribute to those men who died."

Play hard every play. Hug someone you love. Call old friends. Leave no regrets. Scream loud when the joy hits you. Dunk the basketball hard, if you're young and tall and can do it. And if you can't dunk, well, keep leaping.

Life does go on. You just might dunk tomorrow.

— Feb. 6, 2001

BASEBALL'S TOUGHEST PITCHER

ATLANTA — Joe Torre knew the answer. He knew exactly what his pitcher, David Cone, would say. Torre asked anyway. Then, he asked again. Torre had to ask since he was the New York Yankees manager and all, and also this was the World Series, and the bases were loaded, and the Yankees led by one run, and the Atlanta Braves were ready for a big inning, and Fred McGriff, Atlanta's best hitter, was coming up.

Torre had to ask.

"You want to pitch to him?" Torre asked David Cone.

"Yes," Cone said.

"You feel OK?" Torre asked him.

"Yes," Cone said.

"You sure?" Torre asked him.

"Yes," Cone said.

Joe Torre knew these answers were coming. Everybody knew. This is David Cone. The guy beat the Texas Rangers with an aneurysm blocking circulation to his pitching hand. The guy came back from that aneurysm in a couple of short months and threw seven no-hit innings in his first start.

"He's not going to give in," Braves manager Bobby Cox would say, this being everybody's scouting report on baseball's toughest pitcher.

Then, toughness is only one part. Cone had not really been the same since that mini no-hitter. Cone once overwhelmed hitters with all the exploding sliders and angry fastballs. No more. Tuesday he was magnificent, but it was all a bluff. Cone bewitched the Braves with some candy assortment of pitches, none of them particularly fast. He threw some bad pitches, which the Braves barely missed, and some good pitches, which the Braves barely missed.

"I knew it would be like that," Cone would say later. "I knew I wasn't going to be able to throw nine shutout innings."

Now, he was in the sixth inning, and he had walked two guys, he had given up a hit, the bases were loaded, his arm was sluggish, and Yankees fans screamed for a relief pitcher, and Joe Torre was standing so close.

"The experience I have had with Joe is that he waits and talks to you before deciding what to do," Cone would say later. "He looks you in the eye and tries to get a read ... That's part of the specialness of Joe."

This was one of those sports moments. Torre was begging Cone to be honest. He had Mariano Rivera, the best middle reliever in baseball, all warmed up. He had his left-handed reliever, Graeme Lloyd, all warmed up. And he needed this game. Oh, this team needed it badly. The Braves were up by two games, and if the Yankees lost they would certainly be swept away, a World Series footnote. Joe Torre had waited his whole life for this World Series. He had longed for this, prayed for this, and it just could not end quietly.

Torre looked hard in Cone's eyes, glaring in like one of those old horror-movie doctors who want to hypnotize the patient.

"It's very important," Torre said. "Are you OK?"

"I'm fine," David Cone said.

"It's very important," Torre said again.

"I'm fine," David Cone said again. "I'm strong."

Cone's eyes stood firm. Torre believed him. "I trust David Cone very much," Torre said, and he walked slowly back to the dugout, entrusting everything to David Cone.

Cone stared down McGriff. He battled with him. He threw a high fastball, the kind of pitch McGriff likes to drive, only this time McGriff popped it up. The crisis was over. Torre pumped his fist. Cone stomped the mound with his foot. He left after the sixth inning of a game the Yankees would win 5-2, and this thing is a World Series again.

And moments after the game ended, someone would ask Cone what exactly happened in that conversation with Torre.

"Well, he got as close as he could to me," Cone would say. "And he implored me to tell him the truth."

Then, David Cone would smile softly and turn away his head. The Yankees had won. McGriff had flied out. The ending was a happy one.

Cone spoke again.

"And I did my best to lie to him," Cone said.

— Oct. 23, 1996

THE ART OF SCOUTING

There's a committee meeting in the Senate these days looking into what's wrong with baseball. Actually, it's a subcommittee. They call it, deep breath, the "Senate Judiciary Committee's subcommittee on antitrust, business rights and competitions."

Yeah, like these people are going to solve what's wrong with baseball.

Thing is, any fan can tell you what's wrong with the game.

There are too many Scott Borases. Too many Albert Belles. Too many Peter Angeloses. There are too many late-night World Series games, too many autograph shows, too many strikes called balls, too many strikes called by the union, too many kids buying baseball cards as "investments."

There are too many lousy pitchers, too many greedy owners, too many teams in Florida, too many arbitration cases, too many players who want to "play for a winner," too many fans who, on opening day, have no real hope of their team winning.

And there just aren't enough Art Stewarts.

There's only one way to tell the story of Art Stewart, and that's with a whole lot of little stories. Art Stewart, a scout, scouting director and now a senior adviser for the Kansas City Royals, has been around baseball more than 50 years. He has a million stories. Trouble is, his stories bounce around like kids on the dance floor.

He starts one story, hops to another, bounces back, jumps to a third story, slips into a fourth, asks "Where was I?" The phone rings. And you start all over again.

At the end of the day, your notes are a hopeless jumble.

Tripleheaders in the snow.

Baseball in cornfields.

Bo Jackson.

Ball Four.

Oh yeah, they let air out of tires.

Chicago Yankees.

Wife-swapping.

Radar guns.

Tryout camps.

The one that got away.

No, you never know what you'll find in there. Sometimes you find a quote in full, and it's like finding a complete set of dinosaur bones intact.

"You have something inside you," Art Stewart says. "It's that feeling, when you see a player that has it all. Your whole body can feel it. The hairs on your arm stand up. Your heart beats faster.

"Nothing in the world like that, I'm telling you. As long as I've got my health, I want to be around the game. Once you've had that feeling, you want it again and again."

*   *   *

Art Stewart was hired as a New York Yankees scout by legendary old Yankees scout Lou Maguolo in 1953. And here's the only thing Lou told him: "Keep your eyes open. Keep your ears open. Keep your mouth shut."

For emphasis, Maguolo zipped his mouth. That was Stewart's introduction into professional-baseball scouting. And if it sounds like the same spiel they give kids entering, say, the Mafia or the CIA, well, that's about right. Scouting baseball in Chicago was not for the weak of heart. We'll get back to that later.

Stewart had been a fair ballplayer himself in Chicago in the 1940s. Here, we'll let the scout scout himself: "I was a small second baseman. Pretty good fielder. Could run like heck."

A few pro teams showed interest, but Stewart's father died when he was 5, and his mother scrubbed floors, and it was no time for crazy pipe dreams. He did the right thing. He got a job with the Chicago parks department. And on weekends, because baseball was still inside him, he played for a few bucks on a team he bizarrely — and sacrilegiously — called the Chicago Yankees.

"I liked pinstripes," Art says, by way of explanation. "Best uniform you can have. Makes the players look big."

He would travel all over Chicago, looking everywhere for players to play for his Chicago Yankees. He didn't know he was scouting, not until Lou Maguolo found him and hired him and made him take the sacred oath of scouting.

*   *   *

Jim Bouton was the first one to get Art Stewart's heart pumping. Bouton was a good little high school pitcher in Chicago. Some scouts thought he was too small, too frail, too much of a thinker. But Stewart saw that arm, and that was that.

He recruited Bouton to his Chicago Yankees. By then, Stewart was scouting for the real Yankees, and as a result his players were wearing priceless hand-me-down uniforms, the same uniforms worn by Mickey Mantle and Yogi Berra and Whitey Ford. How much would those uniforms be worth today? Doesn't matter - Stewart had the "NY" ripped off the heart of those uniforms and had a "CY" for Chicago Yankees sewn in its place.

"How stupid was that?" he asks.

You see how Art Stewart stories meander? Back to Jim Bouton. Art got him to play for his Chicago Yankees, but he did not want any of the other area scouts to see him pitch. So, all summer long, Art had Bouton pitch in penitentiaries. Even tough old Chicago scouts would not follow ballplayers into prison.

But Stewart could not sign him with the real Yankees. Bouton went to college, and the other scouts finally did see him, and they liked him, and a bidding war was in the works. Stewart did not want that. So he called Bouton's dad, and said plainly: "Forget everyone else. You want your son to play for the New York Yankees?" And Bouton's dad said: "Yes, I do. Come over for Thanksgiving dinner."

Art Stewart signed his very first player, Jim Bouton, at the dinner table, over turkey and stuffing. The story goes on, of course. Bouton was a 20-game winner for the Yankees, but he's best known for writing the classic *Ball Four*, which is about to be released again as a 30th-anniversary edition.

"I'm on page 39," Stewart says. Only it's page 41 in the paperback version.

*   *   *

A good scout in Chicago always wore a coat. No matter how warm it was. A good scout knew that he might get into a prospect's house to meet the parents. And what you did was take off the coat, knock the phone off the hook and cover the phone with your coat. That way, no other scout could call and interrupt your pitch.

Scouting was different then. It was personal. You got to know the parents, the girlfriends, the family doctor, the family priest, the local rabbi. And it was ruthless. When Stewart first started, the great old Cardinals scout Jim Kauffman told him that a big game had been moved across town. Stewart thanked him, rushed across town and found himself at an empty field that had not been used in, quite possibly, 2,000 years. That was Chicago scouting.

Everything was fair game. Art never went so far as to let air out of the tires like some scouts did, but he became famous for the rainout gag, where he would tell scouts that a game had been rained out (or snowed out), and he pretended to go home. He came back later, of course, because as any good scout knew, no game ever really got rained out in Chicago back then.

OK, so Mike Jurewicz was a player he loved. Only Art was up against one of the scouting greats, Phil Gallavin, who was famous for sneaking players out in the middle of games and flying them to Baltimore for a tryout. Anytime a plane flew overhead, scouts would mourn, "Wonder who Gallavin's got this time?"

Well, Gallavin got to meet with the Jurewicz family first. It was late at night, and Stewart sat in his car outside the house. Finally, he couldn't take it. He wandered to the back of the house just to make sure Gallavin had not slipped out with the kid. Stewart saw the door to the basement was open.

"Well," Art says now, his face a little red, "you have to understand, it was a different time. You would do anything to get these players."

Sure, he sneaked through the door, into the basement, and he listened to every word Phil Gallavin said to the family. He heard the offer. And then, he rushed outside, to the front yard, and pretended like he had been standing there all along.

Then, he walked in, threw his coat over the phone and signed Mike Jurewicz. And even though Jurewicz never panned out, he was the youngest man ever to pitch for the New York Yankees, which is something.

*　　　*　　　*

Donna walked into a ballpark in 1961 — and it wasn't just any game. It was the Elgin, a semipro baseball tournament in Chicago, which means you had to be some kind of baseball fan to be there. She walked in, and the great scout, Nick Kamzic, noticed her and started chatting her up. He told her as an opening line that he worked for the Milwaukee Braves, and she said: "There's only one team. The New York Yankees."

And Kamzic, knowing he was licked, pointed out Art Stewart and said: "Well, that right there is the scout for the New York Yankees."

Six months later, Donna and Art were married. Nick Kamzic was the best man.

*　　　*　　　*

Art Stewart saw Rick Reichardt play baseball at a high school at Wisconsin, and he couldn't let go. He just couldn't. Reichardt's dad told every scout that Rick was going to college, no matter what, but Art just wouldn't take no for an answer. He had never seen a ballplayer like Rick Reichardt. It would be more than 20 years before he would see one like him again.

This kid could do everything. He played basketball one year: All-State. Football one year: All-State. And he was born for baseball. All the other scouts backed away, but Art could not. He pleaded with the kid to come to New York. Finally Reichardt agreed, and the Yankees treated him to dinner at the Stork Club, got him tickets to "Hello, Dolly" and took him through the bright lights of Times

Square. "I've never wanted to sign a kid so badly," Art says.

The kid went on to play at the University at Wisconsin anyway.

A couple of years later, California owner Gene Autry unloaded $205,000 on Reichardt — a deal so obscene it helped bring about the amateur draft — but by then Stewart could see the kid wasn't quite the same. Early in his pro career, Reichardt had an illness and had a kidney removed. He spent parts of 11 years in the big leagues, but never quite became a star.

At the end, Rick Reichardt played for the Royals. Art Stewart would go to the ballpark and watch him and dream of what might have been.

*   *   *

OK, so Art Stewart got this tip about a lefty with a great fastball. He went up to this cornfield in northern Illinois to watch him pitch. You should know Art well enough by now to know he would have gone to northern Fiji to watch a kid pitch, if he could drive there.

Most of the time, these tips went bad. But sure enough, there in the cornfield, he watched Fritz Peterson throw beautiful fastballs. He didn't use a radar gun — old scouts didn't need radar guns. Art saw what he needed to see, called the Yankees, and said: "We need this kid."

Art brought the kid with him to Chicago when the Yankees were in town, and signed him right there, in the visiting clubhouse. Peterson won 20 for the Yankees one year, but really was much better known for 1973, when he and Yankees teammate Mike Kekich actually traded wives. Kekich soon divorced Peterson's former wife, but Fritz Peterson and the former Susanne Kekich are still married.

"I signed baseball's most successful wife-swapper," Stewart says with glee.

*   *   *

The first year after Art Stewart joined the Royals, he held 140 tryout camps across America. Royals owner Ewing Kauffman had this idea about finding good athletes — football players, soccer stars, gymnasts, whatever — and teaching them how to play baseball. Lots of people thought Kauffman was crazy. Some still do. Art Stewart loved the idea. And he believed.

So every day, through spring, summer and fall, Stewart would travel to another town, and watch kids play baseball. He saw some good players. Big Tom Bruno pitched for three teams in the major leagues. Sheldon Mallory made it up to Oakland for a year. There were others.

Mostly, though, the kids who showed up weren't football players or soccer stars or any of that. They were kids who wanted so badly to play baseball, kids with baseball dreams but not enough arm, not enough size, not enough speed. Some of them weren't even kids — they were 27 or 28 years old, and they would lie about their age, though Art could always tell.

Some would travel from hundreds of miles away. Some slept in their cars the night before the tryout. Art felt how much they wanted to play. So this is what Art would do: He would keep them around, even though he could tell at the first glance that they had no chance. He would keep them around, and at the end he would pull them aside and say, very softly: "I really wish I could bring you with me. You've got the heart of a baseball player."

And then, he would head off to the next town.

*　　　*　　　*

When Art first joined the Royals, it was very hard on Donna, of course. She had been a Yankees fan all her life. She had this beautiful embroidered New York Yankees rug they had found down in Puerto Rico one year, and it was the centerpiece of the house.

She had a hard time with this Royals thing at first. But one day, about a year after Art joined the Royals, he went on the road for a scouting trip. He came back home, and saw that the entire den was redone in royal blue and gold. The Yankees rug was gone. And for nearly 30 years, Donna Stewart has been the second biggest Royals fan on earth, behind only Art himself.

*　　　*　　　*

Art Stewart saw only three players who got him so excited that he nearly fainted. One was Mickey Mantle, but that was after he was already with the Yankees. The second was, of course, Rick Reichardt as a high school kid in Wisconsin. And the third was Bo Jackson.

To this day, he's not sure why he drafted Bo Jackson. Everybody knew Jackson was going to play football. He was the first pick in the NFL draft. But, you know, Art was never one to let go of dreams, so he drafted Jackson. And, of course, Bo did play for the Royals. And he did such amazing things that even now, all these years later, Art Stewart still wonders how great Bo might have been had he not dislocated his hip in a football game.

"I know there are people who say he peaked, but they're wrong, the guy was getting better every day," Stewart says. "He was like Mantle before his leg got wrecked. He stole (around) 30 bases without knowing how to steal bases. He hit 30 home runs on sheer power. If he had kept playing, he had a chance to be the greatest player who ever lived. I really mean that."

Stewart is known for this kind of talk, of course. When he loves a player, he loves a player. He might walk up to you before a game and say: "This pitcher here, he throws 95 and he's got some kind of breaking ball." Then you watch the pitcher, and he actually throws 88 with a curveball that hangs like the Mona Lisa. Stewart sees players with love.

And Bo is his great love. To this day, the prized photograph in his amazing baseball basement is one of Bo Jackson, the player who could have been immortal.

"You go out there to watch baseball every day," he says, "in the hope and dream of seeing another Bo Jackson."

*   *   *

Oh, Art has a million more stories, about Denny McLain and Marvell Wynne and the day he signed Kevin Seitzer by a cornfield in Nebraska and the first time he saw George Brett, and the time Whitey Ford ... but you can't go on forever.

Or maybe you can. You can still see Art Stewart behind home plate, timing fastballs (he uses a radar gun now — hey, he's getting older), marking down pitches, clocking batters to first base. He has no intention of giving up the game, not as long as he's healthy and sharp, and everyone will tell you he's still healthy and sharp.

"Art's a legend," longtime scout Brian Murphy says.

"He remembers names and places better than anyone I know," Royals chief operating officer Herk Robinson says. "He's really a special guy."

"You look at this Royals team, you're looking at Art Stewart's players," Royals general manager Allard Baird says. "He drafted Mike Sweeney and Johnny Damon and Joe Randa and Carlos Beltran and these guys. This is his team."

Stewart feels sad sometimes about what has happened to his game. It's not fun like it used to be. Scouts don't hide in basements anymore. They don't get to know the families. It's not personal. Everything is agents and money and signing bonuses and, uh, it gives him a headache to think about it.

But, he says, once the game begins, all that goes away, and it's still fastballs and line drives and shortstops moving hard to their left. He still gets that feeling inside watching the game. It has been his life for 50 years, and, God willing, it will be his life for 50 more, because baseball needs Art Stewart, now more than ever.

"I'll be out there," he says. "You never know what you'll find out there tomorrow. Somebody found Ty Cobb, right?"

He laughs. Ah, you never know. Maybe tomorrow, Art Stewart will find Bo Jackson all over again. You know he will be looking.

— Dec. 3, 2000

MARCH MADNESS: THE BEST OF TIMES

O KLAHOMA CITY — Here is March in 2.5 seconds. You don't
care about Valparaiso. You don't know where it is. You don't
care about Mississippi. You've been there.

You don't know any of these players. You don't know any of
their traditions. The Mississippi band plays 23 different versions of
"Dixie." The Valparaiso mascot, a Crusader, looks exactly like the
"Pizza Pizza," Little Caesar's guy. He hardly looks ready for a holy
war.

So, you couldn't possibly care less about what's going on, except
it's March, and there are 2.5 seconds left, and Mississippi leads by
two, and Valparaiso has the basketball.

The guy throwing it in for Valparaiso, Jamie Sykes, is a minor-
league baseball player. He has a great arm. He's also very small.
He's listed at 5 feet 11, but out here he looks no bigger than Webster
from the old television show. Mississippi's Keith Carter jumps up
and down in front of Sykes. He's listed at 6-4. He looks about as big
as the Westin hotel.

"I tried to look over him," Sykes would say. "I could see about
as high as his face."

Sykes, though, has that strong arm, and he somehow throws the
ball, baseball style, over Carter, toward midcourt. Everybody goes
for the ball. One of the players jumping for the ball, Mississippi's
Ansu Sesay, has just missed two free throws that could have sealed
this game. Sesay is 6-9, a leaper, an athlete, the player of the year in
the Southeastern Conference. He wants the ball, wants to put an end
to this.

Valparaiso's Bill Jenkins jumps higher. He has played four

years at Valparaiso. He has wanted only to win one NCAA Tournament game. Is that so much? He has watched other schools pull the upset. In 1996, Valparaiso made the tournament for the first time ever; Arizona edged the Crusaders by 39. Last year, Valparaiso led Boston College with 7 minutes left and collapsed in those last 7 minutes, losing 73-66.

Jenkins jumps higher, reaches his hands above all the other hands, catches the ball and then sees Bryce Drew standing alone. What's Bryce Drew doing alone? Jenkins flips the ball to Drew, the coach's son, the team's best shooter, the kid who his whole life has practiced the last-second shot.

"We have a court in our backyard," coach Homer Drew would say. "And as long as I can remember, Bryce would shoot the last-second shot."

Bryce Drew catches the ball, leans forward as if he's stretching for the basket, and he tries to guide the ball toward the basket. He shoots it short. The ball has no chance of getting in the basket. He knows it.

"I definitely felt I didn't get enough on it," he would say.

His father knows it. "I saw what everybody else saw," Homer Drew would say. "The ball was short."

All the people in the building can see the ball is short, and they let out their breath, they wait to see the ball clank off the front rim, a valiant effort, only then the ball does something kind of funny. It goes in. It scrapes the top of the rim, drops in the basket, like a golf putt rammed into the hole. Everybody gasps together. Then, a roar builds, some crazy mix of Valparaiso's wild joy and Mississippi's wild shock.

"An angel," Homer Drew would say, "directed it over the rim."

And suddenly you care about everything. The Crusader falls

down and kicks his legs around, the Ole Miss mascot, a Colonel Sanders-looking guy, slams his cane. Cheerleaders hug, Bryce Drew prays, Ansu Sesay slumps his shoulders and disappears into the sound.

"My tears are not dry yet," Homer Drew would say, laughing.

"I was hoping he didn't make it, but he did," Sesay would say, not laughing.

"I think divine intervention raised that ball over the rim," Bryce Drew would say.

"It's hard to lose on a last-second shot," Mississippi's Jon Contell would say.

And with that the winners go off to celebrate, the losers off to cry, and the roar echoes and vibrates through Oklahoma City. Everybody cares now. March has arrived. It's still the best sports month of the year.

— **March 14, 1998**

THE LAST
OF THE DANGEROUS MEN

Tom Wolfe wrote once that every airline pilot in America sounds at least a little bit like Chuck Yeager, that American original, the first pilot to break the sound barrier. It is true.

And every NASCAR fan sounds at least a little bit like Dale Earnhardt.

Do you hear them? They are from Los Angeles and Trenton and Houston and Baltimore and Kansas City, but they all have a North Carolina twang in their voices, as if they just walked out of R&R Barbecue there in the heart of Kannapolis. Here, in the aftermath of what might be the most shocking death in American sports history, so many people spill their hearts, on the radio, on television, to strangers, to anyone who will listen.

"What are we going to do without No. 3?" they ask, and they cry, and their voices all sound eerily the same.

Some athletes transcend sports. Michael Jordan was like that. Muhammad Ali. Joe Montana. Took their games to a new level. But Dale Earnhardt was exactly the opposite. He brought racin' back to the simple days, when the money was nothin', and the crowds were nothin', and you drove cars fast for the thrill and the checkered flag.

NASCAR has become big business, with a fat television contract, with huge tracks in giant places like Las Vegas and Chicago and Phoenix, with the biggest sponsors spending the biggest dollars imaginable. This is a billion-dollar industry now. Nobody's out there running on the good dollar of Jake's Gas and Discount Tire.

But, at its heart, racin' is still Junior Johnson haulin' moonshine and dodgin' sheriffs on the dirt roads that twisted through the Appalachian Mountains. Racin' is Richard Petty going out there every single week, and whipping everybody every single week 'cause he had the best car, and then signing autographs until the sun set 'cause he was nothing but a working stiff like everybody else, no better and no worse.

The soul of racin' is in the story of Dale Earnhardt, son of a dirt-track driver in Kannapolis, a little mill town in North Carolina, a good ol' boy who couldn't do much of anything right, except drive a car faster and wilder and closer to the edge than any man alive. He dropped out of school, married young, divorced young, scraped by for a long time on those tiny paychecks that were covered in the dirt of local race tracks.

And for the rest of his life — even after he became a millionaire many times over — it seemed that just about the only place Dale Earnhardt felt alive was out there, on the track, pushing that black No. 3 Chevrolet to the brink of hell, swiping and jolting other cars because he was by God going to get to that checkered flag first.

He was dangerous. That's what draws people to racing in the first place. There's speed and power and noise and courage and freedom. Mostly, though, there's danger. They can talk about safety — and they should do more to protect the drivers — but let's be honest. Auto racing is, at its core, dangerous, and that's its romance. People stopped watching horse racing years ago, and track and field disappears in the non-Olympic years, and when was the last time you watched a good speed-skating competition?

No, it's not the racing. It's the danger. The potential of 3,400-pound cars, engines roaring so loud you can't hear yourself think, all bunched together, hitting the turn at 180 mph, so dangerous. And nobody was more dangerous than Earnhardt. The Intimidator. The man in black. Would wreck his grandmother to win a race. Would sooner knock you into the wall than breathe.

While NASCAR went corporate, while the little tracks in the little towns grew over with weeds, while the small, dark garages were replaced by super warehouses overflowing with parts, Dale Earnhardt connected to another time, a dangerous time, when Fireball Roberts and David Pearson and Bobby Allison and Cale Yarborough went out there and swapped paint and banged bumpers and pressed pedal to metal all day long.

Dale Earnhardt was the last link to those days. That's why he was the most loved, and the most despised and the most everything else. NASCAR drivers today are, technically, as good and courageous as any of those drivers in the past. They drive their cars to the limit, and they react with superhuman reflexes, and death hovers over them just as it has always hovered over the men who race cars. And always will.

But it's not the same.

Faith Hill sings pretty. That doesn't make her Patsy Cline.

Jeff Gordon drives fast. That doesn't make him A.J. Foyt.

Dale Earnhardt was the last of the dangerous men. He was the survivor from that time when bad guys wore black, and drivers slugged each other after wrecks, and everybody felt invincible. In

1997, after a nasty crash at Daytona, Dale Earnhardt climbed out of the ambulance, back into his twisted car and drove it over the blasted finish line. That was Dale Earnhardt.

That was racin'.

"I don't think it will ever be the same," a man named Tom said on the radio, and his voice snarled with a million other sad voices on Monday. Dale Earnhardt died, and, no, racin' never will be the same. Tom was from Hartford, I think, or maybe Boston, but no matter, he sounded a little like the son of a dirt-track driver in the heart of North Carolina. Everybody did on Monday.

— Feb. 20, 2001

FOUR MILLION SHOTS

PISCATAWAY, N.J. — Jackie Stiles has shot a basketball about 4 million times in her life. That's not some crazy exaggeration. She really has taken about 4 million shots in her life. So when the moment came Monday, and Southwest Missouri State trailed, and the crowd screeched, and the gymnasium simmered like a steam bath, and three Rutgers players ran at her, Stiles did what feels as natural to her as singing in the shower.

She stopped, faded a little and swished her soft jump shot.

You don't often get to see greatness up close. Monday night, Jackie Stiles poured in 32 on a Rutgers team that sent waves of defenders at her — strong players, tall players, quick players, cheerleaders, security guards, Sopranos. She led Southwest Missouri State to a 60-53 victory. She willed SMS to the Sweet 16 for the first time since 1993.

More than any of that, she scored 17 points in the last 7 minutes, with the game teetering, the end near, that clutch time when greatness comes out.

Only thing is, when you've shot 4 million shots in your young life, you just don't look at it that way. It's not about greatness. It's about habit. Stiles stopped, faded a little, swished her soft jump shot.

"I'm an instinctive player," she said. "I don't really think about what I'm going to do. I just sort of do it."

*   *   *

Four million shots. It's staggering. That equals 1,000 shots a day since Stiles was 12. And she has shot them in all sorts of places in all sorts of weather. In Kansas wind. In Missouri rain. She has shot over

7-footers like Eric Chenowith, over fiancee Matt Barrett, over a million little girls and a million more tall women.

Most of the time, she simply shot alone.

"I've just seen her work so hard," said her father, Pat. "I'm sitting over there so nervous I can't see straight. But she's calm as can be. This is just what she does. It's second nature to her now."

Rutgers sent a rush of defenders at her Monday. This is how good Jackie Stiles is — Rutgers changed its defense for her. Understand, Rutgers is one of the great defensive teams in America. The Scarlet Knights held Vermont to 29. They shut down Notre Dame's Ruth Riley, perhaps the best player in America. They play inspired defense, led by their inspired coach C. Vivian Stringer, but you know what? They changed for Stiles. That's how good she is.

"I would do it again," Stringer said. Rutgers threw everybody at Stiles. They mixed and matched, they tried the physical Karlita Washington, and they tried the tall and athletic Linda Miles, and they tried superquick Nikki Jett. They played zone and matchup zone and man-to-man and triangle-and-two, and it was all wearing on Stiles, the most prolific scorer in women's NCAA history. She scored one point the first 13 minutes of the second half. She was in foul trouble. She had committed nine turnovers.

Only then, Rutgers led by three, and the 36 banners and five retired jerseys dangled in the gym, and the heaters moaned, and the fans shrieked in piercing New Jersey accents: "This is our house! Go home, Stiles!" Rutgers had not lost on this court all season. Rutgers had not even trailed in the second half all year.

That's when Jackie Stiles decided to go get the ball.

"I thought, 'Go for it,' " she said. "I mean, what did I have to lose? If I had backed off, I would never have been able to live with that. I had to go out giving everything I had."

That's when Rutgers ran three players at her, and Stiles stopped, faded away and swished the shot. The next time down it was a spin, a stop, a fade, a swish. Then she made two free throws. She threw a great pass to Melody Campbell. More free throws. And more free throws. She swished two with 20 seconds left that put the game away.

"I looked at her on the line," Stringer said, "and I thought: 'There's no way she's going to miss. There's no way.' "

Of those 4 million shots, yeah, Stiles probably squeezed in a million free throws at least.

*   *   *

Jackie Stiles can't find the shoes she loves. They're the Cynthia Cooper model, and nobody makes them anymore, and she can't find them anywhere. That's a real problem, because she loves those shoes, loves how they feel on her feet, and she's down to her last pair. Hey, if you know where she can get Cynthia Cooper models, pass it along, because she really needs them.

She loves those shoes. Because Stiles, more than anything, loves routine. She wants everything to feel exactly the same. She wears her hair the same, her clothes the same, her knee pads the same. She eats the same food and goes through the same procedures before games.

You ask: Why? Is she a kook? No. See, Jackie Stiles practices longer and harder than any other player in America. She has shot 4 million shots in her life. So, when it's time, when three players are running at her, and it's the NCAA Tournament, and her family sits in the stands shivering with nerves, and people are yelling at her, she just does what she does.

Stop, fade, swish.

"I don't really think about what I just did," she said. "I was just playing basketball. My teammates did a great job getting me the ball. They set great picks. They believed in me. All I had to do was make the shots."

She smiled.

"I've been doing that all my life."

— **March 20, 2001**

EVERYWHERE, MEMORIES

MANHATTAN, Kan. — Phil Bennett gets out of bed and wanders into the darkness. It is 5:30 in the morning. Phil has, all his life, been an early riser, but before it took discipline, willpower, a little grit to drag himself from a warm bed. From Nancy. He does not sleep much now. He tiptoes softly to the dining-room table. He pulls over the bulging folder of insurance forms and bills. He begins his day.

Everywhere in this house, there are memories of her. He does not know whether that's good or bad. The house looks precisely as Nancy left it that morning three months ago. Dozens of photographs in gold and silver frames crowd together on top of the television. Portraits of the children hang along the walls. The house seems to have been built around the furniture. A coach's wife knows how to set up a home.

Phil tries to concentrate on the insurance forms. He spends so much time these days filling them out and paying bills, it feels as if he has taken a second job. He actually studied business at Texas A&M, but one day, after a rugged statistics test, he realized it was no use. He did not love business. He was a Bennett, and Bennetts become football coaches.

Now, in addition to all the coaching he does as defensive coordinator at Kansas State, he finds himself back in business every morning, sitting under the dining-room chandelier, deciphering fine print, signing documents, making calculations, cutting fat, balancing numbers. There are so many forms, a bottomless pile, each as mysterious and elusive as a Greek poem.

Three months have passed since Nancy Bennett, 41, went

jogging in the early-morning light. Three months since Phil heard the thunder — it sounded like cannon fire — and he drove his car to get her out of the rain. Three months since he drove wildly to the hospital, pushed his way past the guard and then saw her, unconscious, burned, near death. Witnesses said the lightning bolt lifted Nancy Bennett six feet off the ground.

Three months have drifted by since Phil Bennett cried so savagely, friends wondered whether he would make it through the night.

He looks up from the forms and glances at the clock. It is 6 a.m. This was about the time that morning when Nancy left the house. The last thing she said to him was: "See you tonight. I love you." And she kissed him.

*   *   *

Phil Bennett goes to wake up the kids. They seem to be handling things well. Outwardly. He does not know whether that's good or bad. They have always been so resilient, being the son and daughter of a football coach. Sam has moved six times in his 11 years. Maddie, just 9, has moved five.

Life is a wild maze for assistant coaches and their families. To Phil, it sometimes felt as if they had all gone to bed in Ames, Iowa, and awakened in College Station, Texas, sat down for breakfast in Baton Rouge, La., and lunch in Norman, Okla. Everything blurred and bolted past, like they were watching life race and flicker past through the windows of an old station wagon on some bumpy cross-country family vacation.

Then, to be honest, mostly they did not feel that way. Nancy would not let them feel that way. She reminded them all how lucky they were. Every day was an adventure! Any day, their world might change! The exhilaration! How many other children could say they lived in so many places? Well, how many? They could shop at new stores, eat at new restaurants, bike on new streets. And, when the children moaned that it would be hard to make friends, well, posh on that. Nancy would walk across the street, knock on a door, any door. "Hi, I'm Nancy Bennett. Oh, you have a lovely home." Voila. Another friend.

"See?" she told them all. "It's not hard at all."

Phil shakes his son and daughter from sleep. Everything is laid out. Phil Bennett believes in preparation. He is a football coach. The clothes are stretched out. The bathroom schedule is set. The breakfast table is set. Hugs and kisses are written into the itinerary. There's no time for puttering around. Phil expects a little execution from his children in the early morning. He believes deeply in accountability.

"Young lady," he says firmly to Maddie after she gets out of line.

"I don't have to do what you say," she says petulantly. "And you know it, too."

He looks down at her. He knows she's right. She owns him.

*   *   *

There are always letters waiting for Phil Bennett when he arrives at his office in the morning. They arrive even now, short poems and long stories, Bible verses and pressed flowers. There are cards from old friends and gifts from perfect strangers. He reads everything. He rubs his fingers over the small books and enclosed photographs. He cries occasionally. He does not know whether that's good or bad.

"You read the paper," he says, "and you wonder if there are any good people anywhere. They are everywhere. I'm living proof."

Good people. Surely, that's what has kept him going. Every moment of his day seems touched by good people. His fellow coaches take on a little extra work, so quietly they might not know he notices. His neighbors do so many small favors, Phil finds it hard to keep track. Everywhere, every minute, someone pats his back, shakes his hand, wishes him well, offers to help, shares a story, reassures him, it is dizzying.

"The second I begin to lose faith," he says, "someone is there."

More than anybody else, Kansas State coach Bill Snyder has been there. Isn't that remarkable? Phil took the job at Kansas State, and he heard what so many seem to believe: That Bill Snyder, while brilliant, is as distant and cold as the computer voice that tells you to wait for the next available operator. Oh sure, everybody told Phil that. They tell him that still.

But, then, they could not see it was Bill Snyder calming people in the waiting room every one of those 17 days that Nancy clung to life. Yes, it was Bill Snyder talking with the doctors when Phil's mind was so scattered he could not speak. It was Bill who called in the specialists. It was Bill who talked the plainest sense in those ghastly times when Phil Bennett wondered whether all the stars and planets and moons had crashed down on him.

"You take as much time as you need and come back when you feel ready," Bill had told him. But even more important, Bill said, "Whenever you feel ready, come back. We are there for you. Your job is there for you."

Yes, it was Bill who gave him that gift, the greatest gift, the freedom to come back. When Phil did come back, he brought his kids along. Bill Snyder set up a little desk for Maddie near his office. Now, every so often, Maddie will turn to her father and say, "I have to go to the office. I have some work to do with coach Snyder."

*   *   *

Phil Bennett prepares for practice. Messages come in. Karen, a neighbor, plans to take Maddie for a haircut. ("It just looks like she could use one," Karen says.) Val and Clark want to invite the family over for a little chili. Two coaches call to see how he's doing. A card comes in from a former player, now a coach himself. "You taught me about life," it reads.

Phil loves practice. He loves trying to reach his players, clawing his way through the nonsense and junk and grabbing hold of their hearts. Oh, coaching is in the Bennett blood. All three of Phil's brothers coach; two are practically legends in Texas high school football. Coaching, it seems now, was their irresistible destiny.

Their father, Jim Bennett, was always off somewhere, laying pipe in oil fields across America. Their mother, Faye, spent her days working at a department store and refusing to let cancer take her away. There wasn't much money. There wasn't much stability. What they had was football. The Bennett boys played it with a fury.

Phil gave up even more of his heart to coaching than his brothers. They all found homes. Phil shuttled campus to campus, seven so far, spending his time getting fired, finding a new job, getting swept out with a coaching staff, finding a new job again, getting fired again, finding another new job.

"It's a lifestyle," he says, and Phil, less than a week away from his 44th birthday, says he regrets none of it, not one minute of it, because between the hirings and firings, he spent his time teaching football. That's what Bill Snyder knew. Phil had to come back.

"We've talked about that often," Bill Snyder says. "And it seems maybe after Nancy died, he did need to have something else, something to turn to. And it wasn't just to get his mind off it. It helps give that feeling, 'Yes, I can move on. Yes, I can take a step forward. Yes, I can put my life back together.' "

Phil says football has been his therapy. He does not know whether that's good or bad. He just knows that when he's out there with the kids, screaming, prodding and teaching, he does feel alive again. Alive. Like he felt before. Here, on the football field, he reigns. He coaches his attacking, blitzing, free-for-all defense, the same wild defense he has been teaching for almost 20 years. Kids haven't changed, he says. Their clothes change, their hairstyles change, their words change. Deep down, they want leadership. They hunger for discipline. Kids still thirst for a coach to admire.

"The players have rallied around coach Bennett," Kansas State safety Lamar Chapman says. Why? "Because he's so real."

"His emotions are just, boom, right there," says Lynn Allen, wife of Kansas football coach Terry Allen.

"He changed some things around," Kansas State linebacker Mark Simoneau says. "And at first, I thought, 'Hey, what's he doing? We've been pretty successful here.' But look at us now. All I can say is, he was right, and I was wrong."

*   *   *

Phil Bennett watches television with Sam and Maddie. They talk a little about their day during the commercials. This is their time, two hours every evening, just before bedtime. They snuggle together on the couch. They laugh at the silly shows. They hug a lot.

The Bennetts have always been so close. Other coaches might watch their children grow up from the coaches' box — you hear about them all the time — but Phil wanted only to be around Nancy and the children in his spare moments. He had no drinking buddies. He did not play in a weekly poker game.

"People might have thought we were being antisocial," Phil says. "But it wasn't that. It's just that we wanted to be together. It was almost like there was no room for anybody else."

It's like Bill Snyder told Phil: "Don't feel guilty. Some coaches might reflect, 'Why didn't I spend more time with my wife, with my family? Now, I'm going to do those things.' You've always done those things."

Now, though, the time seems more urgent. Phil leaves practice and drives the mile home every day. He plays basketball in the driveway with Sam. They talk about sports, about Kansas State's next opponent, about Sam's next game of football or basketball or whatever. Phil wonders how much he should talk to Sam about Nancy, about the breaks of life, about persevering. Mostly, as fathers and sons do, they just shoot baskets.

"What can I tell him?" Phil asks. "I'm at a loss myself."

Phil tries to get Maddie talking about school or friends or her favorite subject, clothes. She does love clothes. When Maddie found out that they were moving to Manhattan, the first question she asked, the first two questions, in fact, were: "Do they have a Limited Too? How about an Old Navy?"

She was so precocious, so outgoing, so like Nancy. She has grown quieter since all this happened. "It's one of those things where maybe you think, 'If I don't talk about it, maybe it never happened,'" Phil says.

Sometimes, they all visit neighbors. Sometimes, they play games. Usually, though, like tonight, they watch a little TV. Then, they go to the bedrooms, pick out clothes for the next morning. They set up the morning schedule. They go through the various nighttime kisses and hugs. Maddie goes to bed at 9. Sam goes to bed at 9:30.

Quite often, and maybe tonight is one of those nights, Phil stops for a moment after the kids fall asleep. He glances at the photographs on top of the television, the mass of baby photos and family portraits and vacation pictures and candid shots of the kids. In front is a wedding photograph.

"She was pretty, wasn't she?" Phil asks whenever he sees someone looking over that photograph. "How did she marry that guy?"

*   *   *

Phil Bennett watches video. He's obsessed by video. Videotapes are piled everywhere in his office. At night, he drives back to work. He watches tapes in the dark. He looks for weaknesses in opponents. He enjoys the puzzle. Sometimes, a defense must attack. Sometimes, a defense must fall back. Phil Bennett has an innate sense of knowing when to strike, when to retreat.

"He's an amazing coach," Terry Allen says. Through the years, Phil has always improved the defenses he has coached. He is, at his core, an innovator. Kansas State had one of the great defenses in college football before Phil got to Manhattan in February.

"I knew I could improve it," he says. "That's not a knock on anyone. I just knew it. I've never met a good coach who didn't have an ego."

Phil changed the entire defense, added dozens of new twists, gave the Wildcats' defense a complete makeover, this in the worst year of his life. Kansas State is in the top five in America in virtually every defensive category. No team in major-college football has taken the ball away as often.

"Phil has done a remarkable job," says Bob Fello, one of Phil's defensive coaches and a longtime friend. "I don't know that I know anyone who could handle everything the way he has handled it."

Only once did Phil Bennett snap. Kansas State played at Iowa State in October, in Ames, and he felt numb. Phil and Nancy had lived together in Ames when they were young and freshly in love.

Every couple in love has that one heavenly time. For the Bennetts, it was their years in Ames. They talked about everything then — children, religion, dreams, the future and football.

Especially football. After one rough game, she rushed over to him and before saying, "I love you," or "Good job," or anything else, she proclaimed, "Well, I don't know what coverage you were using in the first half, but it took you too long to get out of it."

On the sideline in October, Phil could think only of Nancy. The game rambled on, Iowa State built a huge lead, and Phil Bennett felt in a haze. The Cyclones ran up and down the field. He could only think of her.

"The other coaches saved me," he says. "They made some adjustments. We played better in the second half. And when that game ended, I went into the locker room and cried."

Phil promised himself in that locker room that he would never let that kind of thing happen again. He would be strong. He would endure.

"We talk in football about how the tough survive," Phil says. "But that's not just football."

*   *   *

Phil Bennett lies in bed and stares at the ceiling. It is 1 a.m. It is quiet. He talks to her. To Nancy. He tells her about his day, the children, how the football team is coming around. He feels better talking to her. He does not know whether that's good or bad.

The night before the accident, Nancy had gone to see Bill Snyder speak somewhere. And when she got home, Phil remembers so clearly her being breathlessly happy. She told Phil that when he became a head coach, she hoped he would talk like Bill Snyder. Then, she positively gushed, "This is so wonderful. We can stay here for a long time. This is going so well. You're happy. I'm happy. The kids are happy. We're home."

For a long while after lightning struck, the cruelty was almost too much to take. They were finally home. Why would God take her now? Why? "If you don't watch it," Phil says, "you start to feel sorry for yourself."

He will not let himself feel sorry. "This has happened to so many other people," he says. "And it will happen to so many more. It's happening right now, at this very second … I'm not going to lie to you and say I'm doing great. I'm not. Every single day is a struggle. But we're lucky in so many ways. Look at me. I'm working for the best coach in college football. I live in a special place. People have taken me and my family in. I mean, look around. Nancy was right. We're home."

*   *   *

In the days and weeks after Nancy died, Phil Bennett received thousands of cards, letters and phone calls. One call came from an assistant coach for the New Orleans Saints and a friend of a friend, Carlos Mainord.

When Carlos was a young college coach, his wife died suddenly. He had two young children. He did not know how he could go on. But people are resilient. He did go on. And all these years later, he called Phil Bennett to say, "You will make it." Carlos then told a story about having a dinner with his grown children. They turned to him during the meal and said, "Dad, you did a good job."

Phil Bennett thinks a lot about that these days. The days do repeat, over and over, the same exhausting routine, coaching, family, coaching, medical bills, coaching, putting a heart back together. Bill Snyder says God gave us all 24 hours in a day, and that's enough time, it really is enough time, if you use it all, every minute, every second. Phil Bennett believes.

"I know we have a lot of trials and tribulations ahead," Phil says. "It's a long road. Some days, I miss Nancy so much I don't know what to do. I know the kids feel that way. But we're going to keep going. We're going to keep living.

"And someday, maybe — this is what I hope for — I'll be in a restaurant with Sam and Maddie, maybe their spouses, maybe some grandchildren. And Sam and Maddie will turn to me and say, 'Dad, you did a good job.' "

— Nov. 28, 1999

WE'LL GIVE YOU NINE REASONS

NEW YORK — Scenario No. 1: "I thought it was the ball."

Sunday night in New York, in game two of the World Series, Yankees pitcher Roger Clemens was pitching to Mets catcher Mike Piazza. There's a history there. Back in July, Clemens hit Piazza in the head with a baseball. Clemens said he wasn't trying to hit Piazza in the head.

He didn't elaborate much beyond that.

Maybe he was trying to hit Piazza in the neck.

Whatever the case, Sunday night, Clemens pitched, Piazza hit, the bat shattered. And a huge piece of the bat bounced back to Clemens.

And in the confusion of the moment, Clemens understandably mistook the bat for a baseball. Hey, it could happen. A sharp, long piece of wood can look an awfully lot like a baseball, especially in the lights.

Clemens picked it up. Then, because he had mistaken it for a baseball, he naturally winged the jagged piece of bat in the general direction of Mike Piazza. The bat missed. Not by much, though.

"What's your problem?" Piazza screamed at Clemens.

"I thought it was the ball," Clemens explained.

Scenario No. 2: "He did not see Piazza running."

Sunday night in New York, Clemens was pitching to Piazza. The bat shattered. Clemens picked up a broken piece. At this point, he did not see Piazza running. He was looking at the crowd. He was looking at the ground. He was looking at the bat. He was looking at the sky.

He was looking at you, kid.

Whatever, he was definitely not looking at Piazza. So obviously, he grabbed the bat the way you would a spear, and he threw it as hard as he could. Get away, bat! Only then, as the bat was skipping and tumbling like one of those martial-arts death stars, Clemens suddenly noticed that it was headed right for Piazza, who was running to first base.

"Oh no!" Clemens thought. "What have I done? I never saw him!"

"He did not see Piazza running," Yankees manager Joe Torre said.

Scenario No. 3: "There was no intent."

Sunday night, Clemens pitching, Piazza hitting, bat shattered, yadda yadda yadda, and the sharp fragment of bat ended up in Clemens' hand. At this point, Clemens was thinking about the fragile nature of world peace.

"Gee," Clemens was thinking, "why can't they settle all those problems in the Middle East? I mean, like, we should all able to get along."

It was then that he noticed the bat in his hand, with its sharp edge, and he felt disgusted by it. Pacifist that he is, Clemens violently threw it away. Only then, in horror, did he realize it was headed for Piazza. Clemens spoke a silent prayer, and the bat skipped harmlessly away.

"Why didn't you throw Clemens out of the game?" someone asked home-plate umpire Ed Montague.

"There was no intent," Montague replied.

Scenario 4: "It was a get-it-off-the-field type of thing."

Sunday, Clemens, Piazza, bat shattered, and that sharp piece ended up in Clemens hands. What to do now? He wanted to get the game going again, but how? Clemens pondered the possibilities. He could wait for the bat boy to come out on the field. No! There wasn't time for that!

He could softly toss the bat off the field. But what if the bat didn't make it off the field? What if it stopped in fair territory? That would be embarrassing!

He could throw it as hard as he could off the field! Yes. That was the perfect plan. So, Clemens reared back, and he threw the bat hard into the ground, watched it scurry away. He was mortified when it almost hit Piazza. Oh gosh, he had not thought of the danger! Then, no plan is perfect.

"It was a get-it-off-the-field type of thing," Torre said.

Scenario 5: "I don't know. What do you think?"

Sunday, Clemens, Piazza, bat shattered, Clemens picked up the fractured piece, and he threw it hard at Piazza. Plain and simple.

"Why would he do it?" Torre screamed at reporters after the game. "I want someone to answer me that one question? Why would he do it?"

Top nine reasons why Clemens would do it:

1. He's a jerk.
2. He's a hothead.
3. He lost his mind.
4. He was trying to intimidate Piazza.
5. He doesn't tend to be a "great thinker."
6. He's a jerk.
7. He has a history of doing stupid, spiteful things.
8. He doesn't need a reason. There are a lot of senseless crimes in this world.
9. He's a jerk.

Yes, Clemens threw the bat at Piazza, and the umpires were too chicken to toss him, and Clemens followed by throwing a two-hitter, because in addition to being a jerk, he's one heck of a pitcher.

In any of these scenarios, the Yankees won the game, and now they have a commanding 2-0 lead, and this Subway Series looks over. If the Mets don't win tonight, they're finished for sure. Even if they do win tonight, they might be finished. It's hard to imagine them taking four of five games from a Yankees team that has won 14 straight World Series games.

"Why did Clemens throw the bat?" someone asked Mets manager Bobby Valentine on Monday. This was the most popular question of the day in New York. Why? As if there's some logical reason. Maybe he was making a statement about saving the rain forests. Maybe he saw a rattlesnake and was trying to save Piazza's life. Maybe he has a clinical fear of bats.

Or maybe Clemens just wanted to unnerve the Mets. Maybe that's why he threw at Piazza's head back in July.

Maybe that's why he has a reputation around baseball as a lunatic. Maybe that's why Sunday, he broke all the rules, crossed all lines and threw a jagged baseball bat at Mike Piazza.

Maybe.

"I don't know," Valentine said. "What do you think?"

— Oct. 24, 2000

GEORGE BRETT

His father will be the tough one. George Brett knows that. He sits on the Bermuda sand and practices what he will say about Jack Brett, practices over and over and over and over so the words feel natural, like breathing. Well, let's be honest. Brett practices the words so he won't bawl like a baby.

Lord, Brett does not want to cry today at Cooperstown when

they induct him into baseball's Hall of Fame. There's no crying in baseball. There's surely no crying for George Brett, a man's man, who slid hard into shortstops, who ripped apart anyone who messed with his teammates, who whirled in Kansas City night life. Cry? Bretts do not cry. Bretts do not back down. Bretts play hard. When Jack Brett found out he had cancer, he told his wife and three oldest sons, but he warned them not to tell George.

"He's in the middle of a slump now," Jack Brett said. "He's going through a hard enough time. Wait until he turns it around."

Cry for Jack Brett? No sir, he would not have wanted that. And yet, George Brett can't stop himself. One day in June, he was in his car, driving to some business engagement, and he started thinking about the speech, about Jack, and wouldn't you know it, he started crying like Sally Field right there in the car! On the highway!

People were looking in! Brett was mortified.

"I've got to get the words just right and then practice them again and again, until I'm used to them," Brett says. You bet, this is how Bretts handle things. Everyone knows George showed up first for batting practice; he wore no wimpy batting gloves, either. He felt the bat, twisted it in his palms. He would hit and hit and hit and hit, until his hands hardened, until the blisters crusted, until swinging the bat felt natural, like breathing.

This is just early batting practice again. Brett has spent weeks studying film of past Hall of Famers making Cooperstown speeches. He has rehearsed his own words on the treadmill, in the car, on airplanes, words about baseball and hitting and the people he loved, oh, Charley and Whitey and Quiz and Jamie and Hal and Ethel and Ken and Bobby and John and old Al Zych, the everlasting equipment manager, who still won't tell George how old he is.

But here in Bermuda, he works on the toughest words of all.

George Brett loves the beach. When he was young, he often wandered to the Pacific Ocean instead of practicing baseball. And when he got home, Jack would tear his head off about wasting his life. Yes, here, back on the beach, George tries to come up with words for Dad, the right words, meaningful words, soft words that won't make him cry in front of everybody.

*   *   *

Charley. George Brett never writes out his speeches. He jots down a word, and it sparks a flood of thoughts. Then, he just unloads his heart. He might, for instance, jot down "Charley," and that would, of course, mean Charley Lau, and Brett will be off to 1974, when he had wild hair and was hitting .200 and was scared to death that by morning he would be back in Omaha, making 500 bucks a month.

"Kid," Royals hitting coach Charley Lau said as he sat down next to Brett on a plane ride home. "I want to talk to you."

Brett looked away from Lau's hard eyes. He was just a frightened kid back then. Jack McKeon, the Royals manager, would look down the bench for a pinch hitter, and this kid, Brett, would hide behind Cookie Rojas.

"I didn't want to go in there," Brett says. He believed in the inspiring words of his old pal, Jim Obradovich, a backup tight end for the Tampa Bay Buccaneers.

"George," Obradovich used to tell him, "if I had to play, they would find out that I CAN'T play."

Charley Lau knew all this. He looked so doggone mean, but he had this soft voice and this way of getting inside you. Lau said this: "I've been watching you, George. You can be a good hitter. But it's going to take an awful lot of work. If you give me your heart and soul, I'll make you a great hitter."

Brett nodded. He was ready. He was desperate. The funny part is that Lau worked with Brett for five minutes, five stupid minutes, and Brett started screaming line drives everywhere.

"Hey, I got it!" Brett screamed.

"You don't have anything, Mullet Head," Lau hollered, and together, every day at 4 p.m., they tinkered and adjusted and overhauled that swing. Really, though, Brett was right. He did have it. He banged balls off walls the rest of the season, raising his average to .292. He was thinking .300. That's when McKeon canned Lau, sending Brett into a zero-for-12 freefall.

The slump was temporary; the swing eternal. Lau was back, and then fired. He went to other teams. Hitters loved him, managers did not, and he'd get booted again. That was Lau's destiny. Brett's destiny was to hit for 20 years with that beautiful swing that Charley Lau taught him.

*　　　*　　　*

Kansas City. They used to sit in the clubhouse every night after a game, George Brett and Jamie Quirk, and they would pop a beer or three, and they would talk about the game. And then, every night, one of them would say "You know, I'm pretty tired tonight. I think maybe we should head on home."

That, of course, is when their nights started. George and Jamie never went home. Not ever. He and Quirk would bounce about Westport, drink at the Granfalloon, check out the beautiful women, get checked out themselves, buy drinks, get free drinks, and it was all very alive and very loud and very wild and very together.

"I think people loved having George out on the town all the time," Quirk says. "It made him bigger than life. He was like Kansas City's Joe Namath. People would see him out, and they would pat him on the back. Then, the next day, he would be out there on the field, and everybody in the ballpark would be wondering, 'Gee, I wonder what George did last night.' Then, he would go three for four with a couple of doubles and everybody loved him."

The days of sweet romance between stars and their towns dies now.

Everyone blames free agency — "Players don't stay around anymore," is the melancholy music of talk radio — but truth is, things have gotten too big, too fast.

See, there were no autograph hounds then, no baseball card dealers, no 24-hour sports channels digging for news. The players did not collect luxury cars and hide away in suburban mansions. There was less distance between us all.

Kansas City was just right for a handsome kid who could hit. His manager and friend, Whitey Herzog, taught him how to fish and hunt and said, boldly, plainly, "You are my superstar." He adored his teammates, especially a hard-charging man named Hal McRae who taught him to play the game hard. He had endorsements, business deals. He bought a beautiful home among the trees.

And at night, he and Jamie Quirk never went straight home. It wasn't all innocence, of course. There were near-fights and stormy nights, but it's funny because now, when Brett remembers it, he remembers mostly the people who patted him on the back and said, "Nice game, George," the way they might say "Nice pour" to the bartender. It was like that.

"It was just a special time back then," George Brett says. "I don't think it can ever be like that again."

*   *   *

Baseball. George Brett sort of regrets the way baseball ended for him. He loved baseball so much. He loved the crowds. He loved to chew. He loved to spit. He loved the clubhouses, the jokes, the card games, the crazy bets, the way it felt to throw the ball across the infield.

Most of all, of course, he loved hitting. Oh, the nights were blurs and the days smelled of hotel rooms, but when he scraped his spikes into the dirt, well, the circus stopped. He felt so alive in the batter's box. He would lean back. What was the pitcher going to throw?

Inside curve? He'd rip it down the right-field line. Fastball? Smack that right back at him; flip the cap off his head. Outside changeup? He'd rifle that thing into left, between the two outfielders, all the way to the wall.

Brett loved his wars with pitchers. He would step in and whisper to himself, "You're the greatest hitter in baseball. You're going to kill this guy."

The nerve of the pitcher actually throwing the ball drove Brett into a rage. "How dare you!" he thought. And when he pulled a grounder to second or popped up weakly, he would fume at himself for letting a pitcher — a pitcher! — get the best of him.

You bet he loved it all.

So he always talked about how he wanted it to end. He wanted to hit a ground ball to second and then run like heck to beat out the throw. That, Brett figured, summed up up what the game meant to him.

Some five years later, through, he is not so sure.

"I wish I would have come back for one more season and played for the minimum salary," he says. "I would have given all the money to ALS. You know, played the game for free. Just for the love of it. Go to spring training, try to make the team like a rookie. I think that might have been the way to do it. What do you think?"

You tell him that would have been wonderful. Still it ended so beautifully, with him kissing home plate, his city around him, his fans standing and crying. He nods but his eyes are off somewhere else.

"Yeah," he says. "But one more season. That really would have been something."

*   *   *

Life. Too many of them died. Charley went first. George Brett still remembers going to see his old manager Dick Howser in the hospital, the echo of that World Series dance still ringing in both their ears. Brett was playing third base with one out to go, and he walked over to pitcher Bret Saberhagen and said his well-known words: "Kid, I've waited a long time for this. You better make sure I'm the first one who hugs you or I will beat the ... "

You know, that had been the most special team, that '85 team, and not just because they won it all. No, there was something else.

"Nobody cared about themselves," says Frank White, who hit cleanup in the World Series because there was no one else. "That was a real team."

"You would have a relief pitcher who gave up the tying homer in the ninth and the hitter who won it in the bottom of the inning, and they were both just as happy because we won," Brett says. "That's all that mattered. I always said I would gladly hit .200 if we won, and

I always meant it. But that year, everyone felt that way. Nobody even knew what they were hitting. Nobody knew their ERA. Nobody cared."

Dick Howser was the man who made that happen. Dan Quisenberry called him a distant general — he wasn't much for strategy or heart-to-heart talks — but he had dignity. He had soul. He told those Royals they were the best team, and they believed him. It was that simple.

"We had 25 guys," Brett says, "who believed. I played 20 years. I never was around another team like that."

That team also was touched by tragedy. Dick Howser died of a brain tumor in 1987. Eleven years later, it was relief pitcher Dan Quisenberry who died of the same thing. Brett sobbed softly when he heard Quisenberry had cancer, and he thought about how, whenever he had given up a game-winning run, Quiz told reporters that he had let the team down: The team had won the game; he had lost it. Brett's eyes get misty now when he remembers.

"Quiz," Brett says, and this is his ultimate compliment, "was a teammate."

There was one more. In a hotel room on the road, the phone rang.

"George," Jack Brett said. "I've got cancer."

*   *   *

Dad. People just cannot know how scared George Brett would get.

Before games, he often watched a videotape of himself cracking doubles into gaps, raking low balls up the middle, diving for line drives, stealing bases. He did not watch it to inspire himself.

He watched it to remind himself, again and again, that he was a great ballplayer.

"Every game, I thought I would embarrass myself," he says. "I thought, 'What if a ball goes through my legs? What if I strike out and fall down?' I would look up into the stands and see all those people and think how much it mattered to them. What if I let them down? What if we lose because of me? Every day I thought those things."

All that, of course, came from Jack. George grew up in an ordinary house on a tree-lined street in El Segundo. He had three older brothers who acted pretty much the way older brothers act. His mother, Ethel, offered love and shelter from the storm.

Jack was the storm. He was a financial director for Nissan, but so much of his life was built around his four sons and baseball.

Jack, himself, had not played ball, but he had been a huge Yankees fan in Brooklyn. He wanted his sons to play the game brilliantly.

John had the fire. Ken had it all. Bobby had the brains. Then, there was George.

"We used to just stare, look at him and say, 'Poor George,' " Jack told *Sports Illustrated* almost 20 years ago, "Poor George."

George was the slacker. That's how Jack Brett saw it, plain and simple. George did not work. George did not care. And that infuriated Jack Brett, enraged him. He would kick his youngest son, scream at him, intimidate him. Even now, George Brett can feel the Siberia-cold of those car rides home after he had struck out in a Little League game.

"He would not say a word," George says. "He would just sit there and choke that steering wheel."

George Brett could never please his father, not even at the end.

"I played every single game of my career knowing that if I went 0 for 4 or made an error, my father's entire day would be ruined," Brett says.

The men clashed hard. One day, Ken Brett won a game and also homered. George went zero for three. "You're getting outhit by your brother, and he's a pitcher," Jack screamed over the phone. George went crazy, slammed down the phone, threw stuff against the hotel walls.

George Brett had a lot of rage in him back then. He got in that fight with Willie Wilson, he struck a photographer with his crutch, he took a bat to the toilets in Minnesota.

"I'm not proud of some of the things I did as a ballplayer," he says. "I broke a guy's leg once in a collision. I'm not proud of that. There were times it was too intense for me. There were times when my hunger to win went overboard."

He was Jack Brett's son.

Some years later, the ferociousness inside him calmed a bit.

Once, he chased down a foul pop-up but then rammed into the wall. The ball popped out.

"You telling me you couldn't hold on to that ball?" Jack Brett screamed at him over the phone.

"Dad," George said sweetly, "how many times have you run into a wall while chasing a foul pop-up?"

Jack Brett died in 1992. Only now does George understand how much he is like him. He thinks back to the greatest game he ever played, a 1985 playoff game against Toronto. He hit two home runs, a double, scored the game-winning run, made a brilliant defensive play.

Looking back, though, he remembers one thing. "That double," he says, exactly as Jack Brett might say, "should have been a triple.

"See, I really believe I'm the type of person who had to be pushed constantly," George says. "Dad knew that. He knew just how much I needed to be pushed. No, he wasn't the nicest man in the world. But he taught me a quality of life. I never would have made it to Cooperstown without him. I never would have come close."

George Brett begins to cry just a little. He tells about the last time he talked to Jack Brett. He had gone hitless with a couple of strikeouts. He talked to Jack that night.

"How did you do?" Jack Brett asked.

"I went 0 for 3," George said.

There was silence on the other end. But by then, Jack Brett was too tired to rage, too tired and too sick and too old, and, besides, by then he knew his son was going to Cooperstown. He knew.

"Did you hit the ball hard at least?" Jack finally asked.

"Yeah Dad," George Brett said. "I hit the ball hard."

*　　　*　　　*

Boys. George Brett's three sons — Jackson, Dylan, Robin — they all grow so fast. Little boys always do. They climb on their father, tug at him, beg for Cokes and cotton candy. George says his wife, Leslie, is the easy one; she's the calm one. It takes George's stern voice — his Daddy voice — to get them settled down. These days, George doesn't want to be a coach or a manager or anything like that because he wants to be with his sons. He gets to see them grow. He gets to play catch with them.

"Dylan," George Brett says to his son as he throws, "put your left foot forward when you throw the ball."

Dylan, the 5-year-old, still heaves the baseball flatfooted, as if he's tossing away a banana peel. George shakes his head.

"Dylan," he says a little louder. "Put your left foot forward when you throw the ball."

Dylan gently puts his left food down and throws forward.

"Better," George Brett says. "That's much better."

— July 25, 1999

IV

LOUSY AT RADIO

The grandest moment of my distinguished two-month radio career was no doubt that Tuesday afternoon in early August when the voice of my radio partner, Brooks Melchior, suddenly disappeared. He was in River Falls, Wis., at the time and his microphone had, in technical terms, gone dead or something. Those were the audacious, early days of 1250 AM, a time when it seemed that millions of dollars of sophisticated and delicate radio equipment had been installed by forest animals.

Anyway, Brooks' voice cut off suddenly, and everything was quiet. I mean everything. The whole world was quiet. And I was left with the age-old adventure of filling time that has faced every great radio voice from Walter Winchell to Orson Welles to Mike and the Mad Dog.

Like those men, I rose to face the challenge.

"Uh, you've got to say something," producer Nate Bukaty said through my earphones.

"Say what?" I said into the microphone.

"People can hear you."

"Hear me?" I said into the microphone.

"Yes. Fill time."

"Fill time?" I said into the microphone.

"Go to a commercial."

"Commercial?" I asked into the microphone.

Yes, it was classic and thoughtful radio, up there, I must say humbly, with Edward R. Murrow's "This is London" soliloquy. Still, despite that and weeks of similarly inspired talk, the time has come for me to walk away from radio. Friday was my last show. I feel like I have accomplished everything there is to accomplish in the art form, and it's time to move on to serious literature and human charity and a house with more leaks than the Nixon White House.

Oh yeah. Also I was really, really lousy at radio.

*   *   *

I've never liked my voice. That's natural, of course. Most people hear their own voices, and they cringe. But, by coincidence, I've found that nobody likes my voice. Dogs run howling. When I was 18, I sent a play-by-play baseball tape to a radio personality named Gary Sparber, whose rare talent was that he had to be the nicest person on earth. Gary did a show called, like, "Super Nice Sports Talk," where he earnestly agreed with callers. A caller might say, for instance: "Gary, you are the worst talk show host ever," and he would respond "Excellent point. And by the way, stay on the line, we're giving you a $25 gift certificate to Pizza Hut."

Gary sent me a nice letter, of course, drenched with uplifting sentences like "You will, of course, have to work on your voice," and "Your voice, as you surely realize, needs help." You could tell he wanted to write "You have a better chance of becoming long snapper for the Calgary Stampeders." In the end, sadly, Gary's own rich voice abandoned him after an illness, and he ended up going to New York to sell insurance or some such thing.

Even more sadly, I got a radio show. That's the way it goes in the business. You write two newspaper stories in a row, and inevitably someone offers you a radio show. It's a complete mystery to me.

People have offered me radio shows in three different cities, and, preposterously, they have usually offered cartoon bags of money to go along. One woman offered me a weekly television show. I don't say any of this to brag. I say this because, well, look at me. Would you offer me a show? Is there some television or radio void for balding, chubby guys with screechy voices? Does anyone believe this trend is coming in vogue soon? Who is scouting talent for these people anyway?

I kept saying no, partly because I didn't have the time, mostly because I didn't have any talent whatsoever. Then, something strange and unexpected happened: We bought a beautiful, creaky, sweet, 61-year old house with wallpaper from the Mesozoic Age and ghosts in the attic that used to howl through the night: "This house will cost you a bundle! Whoo! The foundation is cracking! Whoo! Your heating unit will go out tomorrow! Whoo!"

Suddenly, for the money, I could make the time. The lack of talent was their problem.

*   *   *

Friends are so nice. Often, after "The Locker Room," my show with Brooks Melchior, people would heap lavish compliments such as "Well, you didn't swear," or "At least nobody was seriously injured." One particularly dear friend, a groomsman at my wedding for crying out loud, said simply: "That's the worst radio show I've ever heard. And I like talk radio."

Ah, yes. Friends. See, the trouble with radio is that it doesn't stop. You might think this column is stupid — that would be very perceptive of you, by the way — but it ends soon. Radio just keeps going and going, nonstop, forever. There is always more time to fill, more opinions to toss out, more callers, and what happens is that someone like me just keeps talking and talking until something stupid comes out.

Me at 12:15: "Carl Peterson is a tough negotiator."

Me at 12:34: "Carl Peterson is a very tough negotiator."

Me at 12:57: "Carl Peterson is a bully."

Me at 1:15: "Carl Peterson is a jerk."

See? There are people in this town who are good at this stuff. Brooks is good at this stuff. Brooks can, with a straight face, say something like "This show is brought to you by Kansas City's hottest showclub," while I'm in a corner giggling incessantly, like Beavis.

I'm out of the business. It was fun, but I just did not belong. Radio won't be poorer for it, but I will. Those ghosts are still howling up in the attic about busted pipes and cracking paint. They also want to know whether Miles Prentice will ever own the Royals. Maybe, every so often, I will even talk a little sports with them, you know, for old times' sake.

— Oct. 9, 1999

THE WORLD'S FASTEST MAN

SYDNEY — Maurice Greene's head nods in prayer. People have no idea how nervous he is. Yes, they have seen him tooling around town in that Ferrari. The paparazzi have photographed him endlessly with that Australian model. They all think he is so cocky, so sure, so smug; that's what he wants them to think. Fastest man in the world.

They have no idea that, inside, Maurice Greene is so scared. He couldn't eat Friday night. Couldn't sleep. What if he lost this 100-meter race? The thought bubbles and churns in his stomach — he has no answer. What if he lost? There is no answer.

Maurice Greene knows he could not survive losing. Not this race. This is the Olympics. This is everything he has lived for. What if he lost? Greene could tell only a few friends about this terrible dream he has sometimes, the one where he runs a race and then, in the middle, feels himself slowly disappearing. That's what would happen if he lost.

"Please God," he whispers softly.

And he listens for the starter's gun.

Step 1: The start is always the key. Maurice Greene has never been a great starter. "Start well, and you will finish well," his coach, John Smith, often says. But starting at that precise instant when the gun goes off, that's a blend of luck and skill and, more than anything, a gift from above.

It is chilly in Sydney. A fair wind blows into his face. There won't be a good time today. Greene cannot think about that. There's a false start. They are trying to get in Greene's head. He cannot think about that, either. Just the gun. Think gun. Here it is. The gun sounds. Greene lifts his hands and pushes his left leg toward the finish line. Four other runners start better. Three others start worse. For Greene, that is a good start.

Step 2: Steps are small at the beginning of the 100-meter dash. You have to get your body going, like a skier at the top of the mountain. Greene drives forward. On the outside lane, his best friend, Ato Boldon, pulls away.

Step 3: Boldon has that gift for the start. He has never been the world's fastest man. There are other sprinters who whisper that he doesn't have the nerve to be the world's fastest man. Too nice. Too brainy. Too content. "He is the greatest athlete in the world," says the Olympic champion, Linford Christie. "But does he have the will?"

For now, it is Boldon who leads. Maurice Greene stares straight at the ground. But he knows Boldon is leading.

Step 4: Greene grimaces. This is unusual for him. Often when he runs, his face shows no expression. This is an act for the other runners. A poker face. He wants them to believe he runs effortlessly. But there's no point for an act here. These are the Olympics. Greene clenches his teeth.

Step 5: Obadele Thompson in Lane 4 is gone now. It's amazing how much a sprinter can see and hear on the track. Maurice Greene is standing straight up now, and his eyes are wide-open, and he can feel Thompson on his left fall behind him. Thompson, a wonderful runner from Barbados, was supposed to be a threat. No more. Once they fall behind Greene, they don't catch up.

Step 6: Greene takes his stride in synchronicity with USA teammate Jon Drummond, the runner on his right. It's almost as if they're dancing.

Step 7: Again, he steps with Drummond. It was just like the semifinal round, when Drummond had stalked Greene for 80 meters, then backed off, as if to say, "I can run with you, Mo. Just wait for tonight."

Step 8: Drummond pulls ahead now. Boldon is two steps in front. Greene stares hard at the ground, but he can see it all now. He's losing. The wind rushes through his head.

Step 9: Drummond and Boldon pull away further. They are hitting their peak. Greene is not. It's too early. This is the secret he knows. The 100-meter dash is the shortest race at the Olympics, the fastest way to a gold medal, but here, inside the wind, it's a long race. The first ones to burst out always fade at the end. Greene waits.

Step 10: Kim Collins in Lane 7 looks over at Greene and grins. Collins could not be happier. He's already two or three meters behind, but so what? Look at the crowd! Listen to the cheers! He's from St. Kitts and Nevis, two islands which, combined, hold half the number of people who fill Olympic Stadium. He did not expect to be in the finals. He did not expect to be two lanes over from the world's fastest man. What fun! Look at Maurice Greene go!

Step 11: Good-bye Dwain Chambers in Lane 3. As Greene's left foot hits the track, Chambers of Great Britain almost seems to fall backward, as if hit by a burst of wind. Chambers beat Greene twice this year. There was talk that maybe he had a spell over Greene. It was silly talk. Those were meaningless races.

Step 12: In Lane 2, Ghana's Aziz Zakari begins to pull up. He reaches for his hamstring. Greene does not notice.

Step 13: Greene taps his left foot on the track. Bap. Then, he's up again. Like running on hot coals. A scientist figured out that Greene's foot stays on the track for 0.085 seconds, a time too small to imagine. Of the 10 seconds it takes Maurice Greene to run the 100 meters, he's on the ground for less than four. The rest of the time, he's flying.

Step 14: Drummond breaks stride slightly. You wouldn't think another runner would notice that sort of thing, especially in a fast race like this, but that's exactly the kind of thing Greene notices. He sees when runners around him show weakness. He's like a boxer that way. They give an opening, he puts them away. Greene sees Drummond is about to break.

Step 15: Boldon, in the far lane, is not breaking. He runs so smoothly. So easily. Is this the race where Boldon puts it all together? Greene doesn't know. You never know when a man will run the race of his life.

Step 16: Greene looks down at his shoes. They are American flag shoes.

Step 17: Drummond is trying to get back at Greene. They are side by side, but Greene knows a little something. He knows what will happen the next two steps. Greene is beginning to feel the race now.

Step 18: Greene pulls slightly ahead of Drummond.

Step 19: Greene pulls farther ahead of Drummond. Good-bye, Jon Drummond.

Step 20: There are only two now. Maurice Greene and Ato Boldon. The two best friends. They can see each other on the track without actually looking at each other. It's like they can feel each other. Right now, Boldon feels Greene is closing in on him.

Step 21: They are even now. Boldon and Greene stay in the same house at Coogee Beach, and Friday night had been uncomfortable. They could not talk. They could not sleep, either. The house was eerily silent. It's hard, the day before the biggest race of your life, not to be able to talk to your best friend.

Step 22: Greene still stares at the ground. The other runners begin to look up now, toward the finish. They are at full speed. Not Greene. He has a few more steps before he hits 27 miles per hour, his peak speed, the fastest peak speed in all the world.

Step 23: He is moving ahead of Boldon.

Step 24: What a stride. His best of the race. It's as if someone had fast-forwarded Maurice Greene, like a videotape. His left arm, the one with the bulldog tattoo, lifts high. His head begins to rise.

Step 25: Now, Greene begins to break free. He had always wanted to be an NFL player, a running back, like Walter Payton, and this is why, this feeling of daylight, breaking through, nobody can catch you. This is the same feeling.

Step 26: Darren Campbell in Lane 1 turns his head right, looks over at Greene. He knows what all the runners know, all of them except Boldon. They are running for silver.

Step 27: Greene's earring flashes in the stadium lights.

Step 28: Boldon is a full step behind. He can feel himself falling away. What chance does he have now? "We mere mortals run the 100 meters," Boldon often says. "Maurice Greene soars."

Step 29: Greene's head starts to lift up. He's at full speed. Now comes the hard part. The gut part. The last 30 meters. This is when you let out everything you have inside. This is when you reach in there for something to pull you through, something that will take you all the way to the finish. Maurice Greene is the best finisher in the world.

Step 30: It was John Capel, the 200-meter sprinter from the United States, who called Greene a quitter. Said Greene was just looking for an excuse to lose. Greene read that quote over and over again. Muttered it to himself at practice. Repeated it at night, when he could not sleep. Maybe that's what he is using to get him to the finish line: anger.

Step 31: Or maybe it is Atlanta. He went to Atlanta in 1996, sat in the stands, watched Donovan Bailey win gold. Greene felt so sure that was supposed to be his gold medal, though Greene was not a particularly great sprinter then. Something inside him just told him he was supposed to win gold. Maybe that's what drives him now.

Step 32: He opens his mouth, takes in a big breath of air. His eyes glance up to the heavens. Maybe it's faith that pushes him to the finish.

Step 33: Greene pumps his right hand in the air. His fingers are straight out so you can see all five. He blinks.

Step 34: The pain is coming hard now, in waves, every step hurts a little more. Greene bites his lip. He likes this pain, though, because it tells him the race is almost over. Just 12 more steps, he tells himself.

Step 35: Boldon will not yield. He's a step behind Greene, but he refuses to fall back any further. Maybe he can catch him in the last few meters. Sure, Boldon knows, better than anyone, that nobody catches Maurice Greene from behind. But, these are the Olympics.

Step 36: The flash bulbs start to pop now. Up in the stands, everyone can see it's Greene's race. They are cheering for him. Outside of America, there is still nothing more glamorous than the fastest man in the world.

Step 37: Greene opens his mouth to gasp for more air.

Step 38: His eyes glance right. He looks for Boldon. Nobody's there.

Step 39: Here comes the finish, the last steps, and Maurice Greene grimaces hard. It's so strange to be this close to your dreams. All his life, Greene thought about this, dreamed about this, the last few steps to Olympic gold. When he ran with his friends in Kansas City, it was always the Olympics, and in his imagination, he could hear the cheers, see the blur of colors — he could feel the glory of those last few steps.

Step 40: Funny thing is, the glory never hurt this much. Greene closes his eyes. His face is all pain.

Step 41: Now, he opens his eyes. He knows. He truly knows. Boldon is gone. Drummond is gone. They are all gone. The stage is his. The world is his.

Step 42: Now, he opens his mouth.

Step 43: And he bundles his right hand in a fist.

Step 44: And he lets out one last scowl of pain, as he sees the flash bulbs pop. From here, the flash bulbs look like stars glittering. He can begin to hear the crowd, too. During the race, their cheers are lost in the wind, but now he can begin to hear the shrieks, the clapping, the stomping. It's like he's coming out of a tunnel.

Step 45: Greene's eyes get big. This is the instant. He is a half step away from the Olympic gold medal that has guided and tossed his life ever since he could remember. If only he could freeze this moment forever, like cameras do. If only he could put it in a jewelry box, open it up every so often, feel once again what it is like to be at the finish line, seven men behind you, the world cheering.

Step 46: He crosses the finish line first. Greene glances up at the scoreboard. The time: 9.87. Fast. Nobody else in the world could have run 9.87 into this kind of headwind. Then, nobody else in the world is Olympic champion. Greene raises his finger to indicate he's No. 1. His tongue wags. He screams, "Finally."

Then, he looks up to the sky and says, "Thank you."

And then Maurice Greene puts his hands over his head. Nobody in the world, not even his closest friends, not even his father and mother, not even his coach, nobody could have known how much he needed to win this race. He never could explain it well enough.

Boldon, the silver medalist, wanders over. They hug. Then Greene says, "Let's pray," and the two of them bow down, and they thank God for whatever it is inside that makes them faster than anyone else.

When Maurice Greene was 8 years old, he told his father, Ernest, that he would win an Olympic gold medal someday. "You will have to work hard," Ernest said. "They don't just give out Olympic medals."

"I know," Maurice said. Eighteen years later, Greene kneels and prays on the Olympic Stadium track. Then he stands, gets an American flag to wrap around his body. He walks around with a smile bursting on his face, and Maurice Greene listens to the cheers only an Olympic gold medalist ever hears.

— **Sept. 24, 2000**

MCGWIRE HITS 61

News from the front...Mark McGwire hits 61st home run and ties Roger Maris...A father's birthday present...A son's embrace...A trip around the bases with the greatest home-run hitter alive.

ST. LOUIS — Mark McGwire stepped to the plate in the first inning Monday afternoon, and he felt at ease. His son, Matt, sat in a metal chair near the dugout. McGwire had worried that Matt would miss this because his flight from California came in so late. But Matt made it. Everything was fine.

McGwire could not believe how calm he felt. Sometimes, in the heat and humidity of this home-run chase, he had stepped to the plate, and his heart raced a million beats a second, and his palms felt clammy, and he felt patches of the claustrophobia that has hounded him for years. Monday, he felt serene. He figured it was good sign.

He had never hit a home run off the Chicago Cubs pitcher, Mike Morgan. The first pitch, a slider, zipped high and outside. The second pitch, a fastball, was high also. McGwire figured this was a good sign, too. Morgan, who has been pitching on and off in the major leagues for 20 years, gives up very few home runs because he usually keeps his pitches low. He's vulnerable, though, when his pitches are high.

You see, it's about little things. This is the part McGwire can never get through the heads of the fans and the broadcasters and writers who want him to explain this home-run thing as a big, sweeping assault on history. They always want him to talk about the big picture, the significance, the immense pressure.

No. The chase of the home-run record, like all great things, is about small moments. McGwire expected Morgan to throw another fastball a bit too high. Morgan threw that high fastball. McGwire tattooed it 430 feet down the left-field line, his 61st home run, tying Roger Maris for the most ever hit in one season.

For an instant, only McGwire knew what had happened. The ball, crushed, headed for the left-field stands, and it began to hook back toward the foul pole, and for a moment, Morgan thought it might go foul. The fans thought it might go foul. McGwire knew. He raised his arms in the air. "I hit this one too high," he would say. "I knew it would stay fair."

He ran halfway to first with his arms in the air, until he saw the ball clank off the Stadium Club window. Oh, what they had to be thinking inside that air-conditioned box. "OPEN THE WINDOW." The ball bounced back into the crowd, plopped off a half-dozen hands, settled under the chair of a St. Louis catering manager, Mike Davidson, who sat in his brother-in-law's seat. The police rushed in to protect him and the baseball.

In that moment, Cardinals announcer Jack Buck said, "Flight 61 headed for Planet Maris."

In that moment, Roger Maris' four sons clapped politely.

In that moment, fans rushed for the concourse to buy programs.

At first base, McGwire high-fived Cubs first baseman Mark Grace. Everybody roots for McGwire. When Roger Maris hit his 61st home run, passing Babe Ruth, no member of the opposing team offered him a handshake. He trotted the bases alone. Thirty-seven years later, his sons would remember that.

"I'm sure Mark will get congratulations from the other team," Roger Jr. would say.

So, the Cubs screamed to McGwire as he jogged by, and in right field Sammy Sosa clapped into his glove, and McGwire touched second and turned to third. Chicago's Gary Gaetti patted him on the back. St. Louis third-base coach Rene Lachemann bashed forearms with McGwire. They had bashed forearms many times before, in Oakland, when McGwire was young.

"Like the old days," McGwire would say.

He had never let his mind wander during his home-run trots. "I don't have time to think about stuff out there," he had said. But in this trot, as he headed home, his mind wandered. He thought of his father, John, who turned 61 on Monday. How about that good sign? McGwire looked up in the stands for his father. He saw thousands of red and white shirts shaking. He heard a blur of cheers.

"I saw him round the bases," his old college coach, Rod Dedeaux, would say. "And I thought I was going to start crying."

McGwire stomped his right foot on home plate. He bumped fists with Ray Lankford and then punched him lightly in the stomach, the new McGwire home-run celebration. Then, he saw Matt, picked him up, looked in those eyes. Matt chuckled but did not say anything. There was nothing in words that a 10-year-old boy could add to this.

"I know what he was thinking," McGwire would say.

Then, McGwire put down his son, and, like a man who had just won an Oscar, he tried to think of all the things he needed to do. He pointed to the sky, his nod to the man upstairs. He pointed to his father and said, "Happy Birthday, Dad." He looked out to Sosa, who has hit 58 home runs and has been his foil and friend throughout this home-run chase. He saluted the Cardinals owners. He saw Roger Maris' sons along the first-base line.

"He tapped his heart," Kevin Maris would say. "Like dad was in his heart."

"I would love to sit down with the Marises," McGwire would say. "And tell them what their father was feeling. Because I think I know."

McGwire's teammates swarmed him then, each of them wanting to touch him, embrace him. McGwire pointed back at his father. He pointed at his son. He pointed at his teammates. He pointed at friends. "I wish I could point at everyone in the world," he would say.

And still, the rush of sound did not soften, still Busch Stadium rocked, and McGwire went into the dugout to hug his manager, Tony La Russa, and take a second for himself, but the sound was too big, and he came out again, blew a kiss, looked at Sosa, pointed to the sky. Still, they did not quiet. McGwire came out again. Still, they did not quiet.

McGwire looked to Matt, and together they smiled.

"That's got to be the best feeling a father can have," McGwire would say.

— **Sept. 8, 1998**

POETRY

MANHATTAN, Kan. — You ask what college football is all about. I'm here to tell you. His name is Cephus Scott. He's 21 years old. He plays defensive back at Kansas State. He's not a starter right now. He's not a particularly great student. He doesn't like school all that much. He never did.

He's a poet, though. You have to listen closely, because Cephus Scott does not know he's a poet. They don't raise poets in the hardest parts of Galveston, Texas. Naw, he's just a thankful kid, you know, thankful though at age 8 he saw his father stabbed and killed, thankful though both of his brothers waste away in jail cells, thankful though the sound of Galveston bullets echo in his ears, thankful though a doctor told him that one good hit could paralyze him for life.

He's thankful because he's here in Manhattan.

He plays college football.

"What do you remember about seeing your father killed?" you ask. Details are sketchy, the whirl of memories of a child now grown, knives, blood, screams. Cephus Scott, now 21, shakes his head. He looks out at KSU Stadium.

He speaks a poem. He does not know that it's a poem.

"I do not think
thoughts
which make me sad.
You know that cheer?
The sound fans make.
That's my father.

My mother is at home.
My father is in the air,
in the cheers."

*   *   *

Would you, as Graddy Scott did, wander into the graveyard late at night to steal clean water so your children could drink? She raised nine kids on a Texas island, Cephus the youngest. Both her oldest sons went to jail because of simmering violence; her six daughters never left town.

That's how it goes in Galveston, in the tough parts, where there is no money, where violence rages, where heroes are drug dealers, where hope is cast away on just making it through the longest nights.

"It's very rough in Galveston," says Chiefs running back Kimble Anders, one of those who got out. "Everything is drugs and gangs. It's especially tough for the younger guys, like Cephus. You don't think about going to college. You think about surviving, you know?"

That's all Cephus Scott thought about.

*   *   *

"I have never dreamed
about flying.
My dreams are real.
I dreamed about college.
I dreamed about playing football.
Look around.
I'm here."

*   *   *

Cephus Scott was 8 when he had carved his plan. He would play college football. That was the way out. That was the way he would reward his mother. She looked so sad. Hopelessness filled those eyes.

Oh, but what if she could see him playing football, in front of 30,000, no, 50,000 or 100,000 people, yeah, 100,000 people, and they would cheer for, well, who else? "CEE-phus," they would chant, and she would be in the stands. What would those eyes look like then? They would be wide open, oh yeah, she deserved that.

She deserved the chance to open those eyes.

"You bet football means more to a young man like Cephus," Kansas State coach Bill Snyder says. "When you've gone through things like that young man has gone through, you need something. You need something to give you hope."

*   *   *

"Have you ever seen the movie
'Ghost'?
That scene where the ghost goes into Whoopi Goldberg?
That's what I want to do.
I want to hit somebody,
so hard,
so hard,
that I go into him."

*   *   *

Cephus Scott's high school coaches at Galveston Ball hated the way he helped up his opponents. "Cephus!" the coaches would yell across the field, "Would you leave that guy on the ground?" They would mumble to each other that the young man needed to be toughened up. Wasn't that what people always said about Cephus Scott, since he was a child?

"He's sensitive," Graddy Scott explains, but others could not understand what made him so soft, so tender, so emotional. Like that day he rushed home and cried and cried after seeing a man hitting a woman in the park or the way he asked, so often, "Would my father be proud of me?"

Even his brothers and sisters would complain to Graddy Scott that she babied her youngest child. The world was tough. The child had to be hardened.

"But they couldn't see it," Graddy Scott says. "He was so independent. So pronounced."

So even as Scott could not help himself from helping up the opponent, he also smashed their helmets sideways. Had they ever seen a guy in Galveston who could hit like that Cephus Scott? He would fly up to the line, unleashed, free, and he would throw himself into runners, causing concussions, cracking helmets, setting school records in some statistic called knockouts.

And, always, he would help up his opponents.

"Next time you help that guy up you're going to play junior-varsity ball!" the coach yelled. Cephus Scott smiled, two gold crowns shining. He was the second-rated defensive back in Texas, fourth in America. He had the grades. He had the test score. The plan was going according to schedule.

*   *   *

"There are a lot of things
I appreciate.
Nothing excites me."
— Cephus Scott, age 9, to his mother

*   *   *

How much does the game mean to you? Your game. Would you give up everything? When doctors looked at Cephus Scott's left shoulder after the injury his senior year in high school, when they saw the slashes and rips in there, they knew he would never play football again. They had some sort of medical term for it. Layman's term: finished. They told Cephus that he was a bright kid, he had a future in other things. Cephus Scott's tears raged so hot, he could not hear.

"He was devastated," Graddy Scott says. "He thought it was all over. I don't like talking about that time. He had prepared his whole life for football, and he was so sad. So disappointed."

A week later, he went back to the doctor and asked to play football. The doctor said no. Two weeks later. Again. He went to another doctor. The doctor said no. He went to another doctor, and, amazingly, he convinced this one to sign a permission slip. Cephus Scott was a football player again. He showed up Friday night, game time, permission slip in hand. He suited up, listened to the crowd, smelled the grass. He could not lift his left arm, but he was a football player again.

See, Cephus Scott got his permission slip by having the third doctor examine his good shoulder.

He did not play, of course. The coach noticed his left arm sagging. The team doctor saw him out there. They took away his uniform. A year would pass. Two years. Doctors kept saying no. How much does the game mean to you? One afternoon, when Cephus Scott's shoulder felt better than ever before, he told the doctor that he was going to play college football.

"But you could be paralyzed," the doctor said.

"Look around you, Doc," Cephus Scott said. "I could get paralyzed walking down the street."

*   *   *

"My brother
sent me a letter
from jail.
He wrote, 'Don't follow in my footsteps.'
I wrote back,
'You're not here.
I see no footsteps.
When you get out,
and you are free,
follow in my footsteps.' "

*   *   *

He had heard of Kansas State because of his brother Lonnie. "We get those Kansas State games on television here," Lonnie had written from his jail cell in Texas. "Go to Kansas State so I can watch you on television."

So when Kansas State linebackers coach Brent Venables called for Scott's roommate at Garden City (Kan.) Community College, Jeff Kelly, Scott could not stop himself.

"You're going to be sorry you didn't recruit me," Scott yelled.

"Hold on a minute there," Venables said. "Aren't you a freshman?"

"I'm a freshman, but I'm going to graduate from here this year, and you will be sorry you didn't give me a chance."

"Hey, settle down a minute."

They recruited him, of course. How could they resist him? This season — his first at Kansas State — Scott started for a while, when safety Lamar Chapman got hurt. Played well. Chapman returned, and Scott was back on the bench, learning. He still likes to hit runners, though things are different in college. You can't just run all over the field, chasing people, knocking them out, helping them up. There are assignments, roles. He learns.

"He's a big-time player," defensive coordinator Mike Stoops says. "Once he learns the system, he can be as good as anybody we have around here."

"He needs to learn," Snyder says. "But he can be special."

All those are just words, though. Scott misses home. His daughter, Angela, lives back in Texas with his fiancee, Tamisha. He calls them all the time. He calls Graddy all the time, too. Anders gave Scott his home number and told him to call whenever he had any problems. Scott shook his head. "I don't have the money to make any more calls," he said. Anders said to call collect.

And it has been hard. All his life, he dreamed about getting here, into college, in front of the big crowds. He planned his escape from Galveston. Now he's here, on the bench. Be patient, they tell him. Patience hurts, though. Earlier this year, Graddy Scott made the long drive from Texas to Manhattan. Cephus Scott barely played. Afterward, she looked for him, wanted to hug him, but she could not find him anywhere. He was hiding away, embarrassed, angry, devastated.

"I let her down," he says. "I can't let her down."

*   *   *

"I need to be on that field.
No matter what.
I need to be on that field.
For my mother.
And my little girl.
For them.
For me.
If not this year,
for sure next year.
Next year, for sure.
I need to be on that field."

*   *   *

You ask the question. What is college football all about? Is it about victories and filled stadiums? Bowl games? Is it about alumni and pride? Is it about academics and a chance at learning? Does it teach life's lessons?

"A young man like Cephus Scott can find family," Snyder says.

"It's a way out," Anders says. "It's a way out of a place like Galveston. I like to go back, visit. I love Galveston. But I had to get out."

"It has been his dream since he was a little, itty-bitty boy," Graddy Scott says. "He's always been focused. Everything was football. College football. It was his plan."

What is college football all about? A 9-year-old boy wrote Cephus Scott this fall. The boy called himself the No. 1 Cephus Scott fan in the world. And in the letter he asked Scott to tell a bit about his life, how he ended up at Kansas State, what drives him to be the football player he has become.

Scott wrote back. He wrote about growing up on an island, how the water looked in Texas, what cheers sound like from the field, how he loves to hit on the football field, how it feels to drape Kansas State purple on the body on game day. He wrote as he speaks. "That boy," Graddy Scott says, a hitch in her voice, "has always spoken his heart."

There was nothing in the letter of the injury or the danger or his brothers or the blood or the man who hit that woman in the park. You ask him why. He speaks a poem. He doesn't know it's a poem.

"Children
don't need to know
about the world.
They need heroes,
you know?
And people who love,
a nice place to play.
And hope.
Football was that for me.
All that.
Without it,
I'd be dead."

— Nov. 27, 1997

PARTNERS IN LIFE

This one's personal. I'm getting married in June. That has nothing to do with sports, I know, nothing at all, but sometimes sports and life cross paths. Sometimes, among the field goals and infield flies and free throws, something beautiful emerges. Wednesday, a bunch of us went to hear Dan Quisenberry. He was a great pitcher once. He has a brain tumor now. It grows.

He sat below a velvet Royals sign, in the basement of Kauffman Stadium, and microphones surrounded him, camera lights shined on him, sportswriters scribbled furiously on note pads, and there were moments when he was laughing, there were moments when he was crying. In those crying moments, his eyes blushed a deep red, and tears trickled from the corners. The Quiz, as he was known in the good years, never brushed away the tears. He is allowed to cry. He is allowed to feel everything.

He talked about how every day means so much to him. He talked about the joy of seeing his children. He talked the thrill of watching a boy pedal a bicycle, legs churning, body bouncing up and down. He talked about inner peace and how he gets tired too quickly and his talks with God. Dan Quisenberry joked with reporters every day of his baseball career. He said he doesn't joke with God.

He talked about prayer and miracles and the odds. He talked about taking walks and taking naps and taking time to see and feel all the little details that had slipped by, unnoticed, all those years, the taste of cold water, the tingle of a cool breeze, the way his old teammate Amos Otis' voice drips Cajun.

He talked about how he doesn't deserve all the people who have prayed.

He talked quietly, but with fire, the same voice he used in the clubhouse after games, the same voice he used to read his poetry. He talked about beating this thing. He knows what the doctors say.

He talked about so many things Wednesday, and I know that's what the news conference was supposed to be about. I know this was the time for Quisenberry to thank everyone for their love and support, to tell everyone that he's at peace, to let them know he's not afraid. This news conference, in a small room of a stadium where Dan Quisenberry saved baseball games, was supposed to be about cancer, about fighting, about Quisenberry telling us, in his own way, that he would be all right.

It wasn't about that, though. For 22 minutes, as he tried to find the sequence of words that could explain life and death and fear and wonder, Dan Quisenberry clenched the hand of his wife, Janie. They have been married for 21 years.

They held hands palm in palm, the way children are supposed to hold on when crossing the street. And they held hands with fingers interlocking, like young lovers. They squeezed hands when the sadness built up. And they caressed hands when talking of good times. Mostly, though, they just held hands, matter of fact, the way couples do, as they talked about their children going on with their lives, as they talked about the radiation treatments that are coming up, as they talked about each other.

"In many ways, these past weeks have been the hardest weeks of our lives," Janie Quisenberry said. "They have been very rough. But they have been sweet too. It's a neat love. Dan and I have been married 21 years, and I hope we get another 21."

She smiled. He smiled. He looked different with his hair shaved. She looked uncomfortable in the camera light. He looked tired. She looked tired. He looked at her. She looked at him. And you know what? This wasn't about cancer or death or chemotherapy or baseball. I'm getting married in June. We were talking the other day, Margo and I, about the wedding vows, what words we should use, what promises we should make, what love means.

"I feel so at peace," Dan Quisenberry was saying. "It's hard to put into words. It's hard to explain."

As he talked, Janie Quisenberry clung to his hand and smiled.

"It's a blessing, in a way," Dan Quisenberry said. Together they answered the last of the questions. Together they thanked all the people who care. Together they walked out, hand in hand, ready to face the darkness, ready for a miracle.

— **Jan. 29, 1998**

A G R A C I O U S L O S E R

BIRMINGHAM, Ala. — The first thing Jacque Vaughn did when the music stopped, when the buzzer sounded, when the career ended, was look for a hand to shake. He turned, found an Arizona player, shook his hand firmly. "Good game," he said softly.

He looked for another hand to shake. This was his final role. For four years, Kansas' Jacque Vaughn has been everything to everybody, he has been point guard and student and leader and role model and star and friend, and now, while the tears rushed around him, he gave his greatest performance. He played the part of the gracious loser.

"What to say?" he asked himself in the terrible minutes after Arizona beat Kansas 85-82 Friday. "What to say?" No words rushed to his mind. No thoughts coursed through his body. Always, he had been able to come up with an answer, always he knew what needed to be said, but now, nothing.

He looked for another hand to shake.

Vaughn could have taken the last three-point shot. The ball was in his hands. Kansas had made a frantic run at Arizona, the Jayhawks had been down by 13, but then they had rushed back with all the fury and anger and force that had been missing all night. "We can win this game," Vaughn screamed at his teammates, his friends. "We have the guys to come back and win."

And he could have taken the last shot. Vaughn had the ball in his hands with a chance to tie. Seconds ticked away. A defender ran at him. He was not sure whether his feet were behind the three-point line. Instinctively, he flicked the ball to Ryan Robertson, like he always had, like he always will, because Jacque Vaughn does the right thing, and that was the right thing to do.

Robertson missed.

Vaughn looked for another hand to shake.

They would all look to him for guidance in the locker room. His teammates. His friends. They always looked to him for an answer, for fury, for comfort, for forgiveness. They had wanted to win this championship for him, especially for him, and now they would look to him with moist eyes, red faces, and they would want him to explain it. "Tell us Jacque, why did this happen?" they would ask.

Still no answers snapped to mind.

He looked for another hand to shake.

Vaughn had not played well. For a few minutes in the first half, he had looked like the All-American, he had darted between defenders, slipped passes into cracks, hit a jumper or two. Then, it faded, he found his shot drifting, he watched those quick Arizona hands slip in front of his passes.

Once, he pulled up from three-point range, threw a shot that fell four feet short, and he howled. He picked up a couple of cheap fouls, bad fouls, and had to come out when the team needed him most.

"It was a bad way to go out," he would say, but those were just mindless words, things you say in your sleep. Those did not touch the pain that bubbled deep down, beneath the daze.

He looked for another hand to shake.

Cheerleaders cried around him. Arizona cheerleaders laughed

and danced. Kansas fans wailed. Arizona fans shrieked. Players hugged, both sides, some in joy, some in agony, and already, the questions rushed about Kansas. What was missing? Why did this happen? Who is to blame? This team had been No. 1, the Jayhawks had been so good, they were supposed to win. They lost.

And Jacque Vaughn could not figure it out. He shook a hand. Shook another hand. His face was blank. His eyes began to go red. People always talk about how the pain does not hit you right away, the numbness hits first, and Vaughn felt the numbness, and his shoulders slumped, and his feet slid along the floor, and he mouthed the words "Good game" again and again.

It was over. He will never play in a Final Four. He will never play on the final Monday night. He will never cut down the last net. All his life, he believed those things would happen, he had written them down in lists, he had scribbled them over and over on pads, he had done all the right things. He had earned it. No. He shook another hand.

"Jacque," the reporters asked, "how do you feel?"

"Sometimes," he said in a whisper, "the best teams do not win."

— **March 22, 1997**

BASEBALL CARDS AND GUM

Mom threw out all my old baseball cards, of course. You can always count on moms to do that. They will call to remind you about daylight-saving time, they will offer you more food no matter how much you've eaten, and they will absolutely throw out your baseball cards when you're looking the other way.

I don't know how many baseball cards Mom threw out, but in memory, there were millions. There were a deluge of George Bretts, Reggie Jacksons, Tom Seavers, Mickey Mantles — hundreds and hundreds of Mickey Mantles, rookie Mantles, Mantles from his prime, Mantles at the end, which is kind of funny because, in fact, I wasn't nearly old enough to collect any Mickey Mantle cards. Memory is a funny thing.

Anyway, I'm not sure what the cards would be worth today, but I would guess somewhere in the neighborhood of, oh, $10.3 million. Mom threw them out. She said they got wet when the basement flooded. Whatever.

Then, it's not the money. It's those cards. I miss them. The feel. The goofy poses. The cartoons on the back. The smell.

And the gum. Oh man, I miss the gum. They don't put gum in baseball cards packs anymore. It's an American tragedy. I miss every single thing about the gum, the way it hardened in the sun, the way the powdered sugar rubbed your tongue raw, the way your jaw ached after chewing for hours, the way the biggest bubbles splattered on your face.

"Remember," baseball fan deluxe Bob Costas was saying, "how you would just wad the gum in your mouth while you were opening the cards?"

Remember? As if it were yesterday. Some people long for Paris in spring or sleds called Rosebud or the first girl they ever kissed. I just want to chew that gum again.

A couple of weeks ago, a miracle happened. On television, there was a story on Topps, the baseball card company. Turns out, in celebration of its 50th anniversary, Topps was releasing a set of Heritage baseball cards, a set of modern cards that look and feel exactly like the cards from 1952. Goofy poses. Fake autographs on the bottom. Silly facts on the back.

And, here's the thing, it would have the gum.

The gum! Yes, the Topps scientists plunged deep into their files, dug up the recipe for the gum ("Take cardboard. Harden. Add too much sugar. Repeat."). They put a stick in every pack.

Here it was — a chance to be young again.

I rushed to the store to buy some of the baseball cards.

And there I got the first lesson of how the world has changed. The store didn't have the cards. They had plenty of baseball cards, but they didn't have these cards. Neither did the second store. The third, fourth and fifth didn't have them either.

No store, in fact, had them.

These were special baseball cards.

*   *   *

How much were baseball cards when you were a kid? I remember them being 15 cents a pack, but that could be wrong. People always exaggerate how cheap things were. You see people in the waiting room of the dentist's office, sometimes, yelling 1950s prices at "The Price Is Right."

"Seven cents for the can of tuna," they yell.

So maybe baseball cards were more than 15 cents. Maybe they were a quarter. Maybe 35 cents. Point is they were priced to move.

And I must have lost track somewhere along the way, because while looking for these Topps cards with the gum, I got sticker shock. Baseball cards these days are $1.99 a pack, $3.50 a pack, $5 a pack. Are you kidding? Yes, it's pathetically fogyish to complain about how expensive things are now, but still, it can't be good when a pack of baseball cards costs more than a pack of cigarettes.

Of course, here's a reason: They keep stuffing more and more stuff inside these packs. Kids don't buy the cards for the cards anymore, no, they buy them for the "special inserts" crammed inside. It's like a kiddie lottery. Buy a pack, you might win an actual Willie Mays autograph or a shred of a baseball used in an actual game or a Jorge Posada card made of solid gold or Chipper Jones' actual thumbnail or tickets for two to outer space or whatever.

"These cards have the Star Ruby inserts," a youngster explained to us, and we didn't even bother to ask what that meant. We just assumed they're putting actual rubies in these packs now. We did ask the boy where we could find the Topps cards with the real gum. He didn't know.

"But," he said, "they're going to cost you."

*   *   *

"Remember the cartoons on the old baseball cards?" Costas was saying. "The cartoons were great. A favorite of theirs was to cite the versatility of those who played two sports. Like Dick Groat was an All-American basketball player at Duke. So the cartoon showed him dribbling a basketball with one hand and having a mitt on the other.

"Or the cartoon would feature someone like Leon Wagner, and it would say, 'Leon belted 37 home runs last year.' And the cartoon would be of an outer rim of the stadium and ball flying to a little kid.

And the kid's saying 'Leon must be up!'

"My favorite was of Lee Maye. He was a singer. So invariably they would have him standing behind some Bing Crosby type microphone, in a suit and tie, with a bat in one hand and musical notes coming out of his mouth. And he would be saying, 'Hope I have hits in the winter and the summer!' "

*   *   *

After the store fiasco, I tried the sports collectible shops. You know, we didn't have sports collectible shops back in the old days. A store selling baseball cards? Why not a store selling just Big Wheels or Silly Putty or PEZ? The very idea was ludicrous.

"We didn't know these cards were worth anything," Tom Watson says. "They were just for fun. Just for us kids."

Anyway, called a dozen or so shops. None had the Topps cards with the gum.

"Too late," one said.

"Just sold my last box," another said.

"They're the hottest cards in years," a third said.

It seems that I wasn't the only one who wanted to go back to childhood. It seems that at first, the packs were selling for about $3 a pack, an outrageous price for eight cards, but the dealers couldn't keep them on the shelf. They raised the prices again and again, but people would not stop buying.

"There's only one place I know where you can get those," a dealer said.

That place, of course, is eBay.

*   *   *

There are spare moments in your life when, if you're lucky, you find all over again that you married just the right person. Maybe it's the morning you go out to your car in a bad mood only to find out that he filled up the car with gasoline the night before. Maybe it's the time you're mowing the lawn and, at precisely the right moment, she brings out lemonade.

For me, one of those moments happened when I said, "Margo, I just spent $177 for a box of baseball cards."

She could have said anything. She would have been right.

She said this: "OK."

Yes, the 24 packs of cards cost me $177. What are you groaning about? It wasn't your money. In case you're wondering, that's $7.38 a pack. That's about 92 cents a card. That's about the biggest ripoff I could ever imagine.

But it did include the gum.

Then, one magical evening, the cards arrived, and we opened them, one by one, champing on the gum, laughing about how silly the players looked in their crazy old fashioned poses, complaining because we kept getting Minnesota Twins. It's always like that. Costas remembers there were always many more Bubba Morton cards than Willie Mays. I remember many more Jack Brohamer cards than Pete Rose. Here, at night, acting like children, it seems as if we kept getting Corey Koskie again and again and again.

*   *   *

Postscript: Since then, the Topps Heritage cards have gone up even higher in price. Some dealers are trying to get $225 for a box now. You don't want to do the math on that. The prices figure to keep climbing, as long as there are people out there who want to feel young for a moment.

So I've told Margo not to throw these cards out — they're

valuable — and she promises she won't. But you know, deep down, she's got that mother gene in her. And when you least expect it, she will throw them out. That will never change. I just better finish the gum before it gets to that.

— **May 10, 2001**

B L O O D   S P O R T

No woman in the United States has ever died boxing. Only one has ever come close. This is the story of Katie Dallam. She almost died shortly after her first fight. This is the story of Sumya Anani. She was the woman who punched relentlessly.

They met briefly before their fight on a Wednesday in December at the Firefighter's Union Hall in St. Joseph. Anani talked about her days as a yoga instructor and massage therapist. Dallam talked about her days as a drug-and-alcohol counselor for the state of Missouri. They spoke nervously, like two women sitting in a dentist's waiting room. Then they walked into the hall, into the roar and the haze, and struck each other for seven minutes.

The two women tapped gloves.

The crowd screeched at the sight of blood.

Dallam collected $300. Anani made $400.

Few saw the ambulance leave the building.

Everybody remembers the details differently, but that's not unusual on nights of tragedy. One remembers shrieks where another recalls silence. One sees fury where another senses calm. Danny Campbell, the boxing promoter, remembers Dallam talking freely when the fight ended. Stephanie Dallam, Katie's sister, remembers only silence and a deadness to her eyes. Katie Dallam herself remembers nothing. She sees the fight only in her painting, with red strokes blushing against canvas.

Then, nobody sees women's boxing itself quite the same way.

*   *   *

Women's boxing yanks a million emotions out of people. It is violence and blood and sex and gimmick and sport blended together so intensely, so furiously that no one can feel one part without tasting another. In a few weeks boxing's biggest promoter, Don King, will put on the first-ever pay-per-view card with all women fighters. Some people laugh. Some are sickened. Some cheer. Some plunk down their money.

In England and other European countries, women's boxing is banned.

In the United States, it swims toward mainstream.

"You have to understand this is not powder-puff stuff," boxing promoter Danny Campbell says. "These girls really fight. That's one of the reasons it is becoming so popular. And it is becoming popular, I tell you.

"Women are not educated boxers, understand? They're still learning the sport. They don't know how to slip punches or block punches. They just stand in front of each other, punch away and the toughest girl wins. Blood flows; you might see a nose broke. They're exciting fights."

Campbell promoted the Anani-Dallam fight of Dec. 11. He says everybody wants to see women's boxing these days, and he gives the same reason every boxing promoter gives: Christy Martin. She fought Ireland's Dierdre Gogarty on the undercard of a Mike Tyson fight, and they stole the night with a six-round spectacle. Martin won the fight, though blood covered her face and body. Soon afterward she glared from the cover of *Sports Illustrated*. Women's boxing had its first legitimate star. Martin now demands a six-figure purse for her fights.

Martin is one extreme. Another is Kansas City's Mary Ortega, who just turned 17, wears braces and says she has her mother's permission to become a professional boxer. She spars with men, hungrily hits the heavy bag and hopes to have her first pro fight in August.

"There are just no opportunities for women in amateur boxing," she says.

Another is Julie Ardwin, who lives in Kansas City, gives physical examinations by day and then throws stiff left jabs under smoky lights. She began fighting a year ago to get in shape. They told her she could make money in this gig. She has won five of six fights. She is tall, intelligent, athletic and stunning.

"A beautiful girl," trainer Joe Gallegos says. "Believe me, that sells."

"Promoters come up to me and say, 'I'm going to make you a star,' " Ardwin says. "And I say, 'How are you going to do that?' They just smile. We're a sideshow. There's not a lot of legitimacy in women's boxing."

Last week Julie Ardwin fought two fights. She won Monday in Kansas City. She was knocked out Thursday in Baton Rouge, La.

"I guess that's pretty stupid, huh?" she says.

*   *   *

The first view of the Anani-Dallam fight comes from ringside. Danny Campbell did not know much about Katie Dallam. In the program the fight was listed this way: Female welterweights, featuring Sumya Anani.

Reporters were told that Dallam was a 26-year-old fighter from Jefferson City. Actually, she was 37, had a master's degree from the University of Missouri and had lived in Columbia her entire life except for the four years she spent in the Air Force. This was her first pro fight. She had been training for six weeks with Gallegos. She had trained as a kick boxer for a while but had never stepped in the ring. Her entire ring experience consisted of one round in the women's portion of a Tough Man contest. She lost.

"(Gallegos) called me and said he was looking for a fight for his girl," says Campbell, who was more interested in Anani, the fighter he promotes still. Anani had been fighting for only six months, but she won all three of her fights. She was 24. She grew up in Kansas City but had briefly been a massage therapist and a blackjack dealer in Jamaica. Campbell called her the Island Girl and the Jamaican Sensation. It was tough narrowing down from there.

Dallam outweighed Anani by 35 pounds. The Missouri State Boxing Commission does not allow boxers to fight out of their weight class unless special permission is granted. It was granted for this fight.

"There are not many women's fighters," Campbell says. "They're pretty lenient about weight differences."

The day before the fight, Dallam received her boxing license. That night, she was in a car wreck serious enough to send her trainer into the hospital.

"She was driving and seemed OK," Gallegos says. "I was covered in blood from head to toe. But then, I'm a bleeder."

Campbell says he was never told about the accident, nor was the Missouri Office of Athletics. After a routine pre-fight physical, the fight went on as planned.

"It was the kind of physical a 90-year-old man could pass," Dallam's sister, Stephanie, says.

"This is absolutely sickening to me," says Tom Moraetes, an amateur boxing trainer in Augusta, Ga., for 24 years and the tournament director for the first-ever amateur women's boxing championships this July. "I can't even believe this fight was sanctioned. She's 37. She's never fought before. She's trained for six weeks. She's in a car wreck. This is the worst of boxing, right here."

The fight began at 9:51 p.m.

Anani wore a yellow sports bra and shorts.

Dallam wore a black, oversized tank top.

Anani began landing punches almost immediately.

"It was an incredible fight," Campbell says. "It was a lot better than I expected it to be. Sumya decided to go toe to toe with the girl. She would just throw so many punches. That other girl was just not in the kind of condition to survive all that later in the fight. She wouldn't go down, though — showed a lot of heart."

Dallam's nose began bleeding less than a minute into the fight. Anani was simply too quick for her. In the cloud of memory from the fight, Dallam would only vaguely recall the first punch, and it seemed like four gloves coming at once. Anani flailed away. In the second round, Anani landed blows time after time to the head, including a four-punch combination to the face. In the third round, people in the crowd screamed for Anani to finish her off. It was a 12-punch flurry to the head in the fourth round that prompted the referee to pause the fight for the first time and give Dallam a standing-eight count. Gallegos threw in the towel.

Dallam remained on her feet the entire fight.

She never stopped trying to fight back.

The videotape shows Anani landed 119 punches to the head. Dallam landed fewer than 40. Because it was a professional bout, neither fighter wore headgear.

When the fight ended, Dallam slumped to her corner. Many things happen at the end of a fight, so many it is hard to keep track. The ringside doctor, C. Daniel Smith, says he briefly checked Dallam, found her responsive and let her go. Katie's sister says the doctor never got up from his seat. Anani says she tried to speak to Dallam but got no response. Stephanie Dallam says her sister's arms were ice-cold.

"She didn't even recognize me," she says.

Gallegos says Dallam didn't feel faint until she reached the dressing room. She asked for an aspirin. She couldn't swallow it. She collapsed.

By the time Dallam reached Heartland Regional Medical Center, her brain bled profusely.

*　　　*　　　*

Stephanie Dallam's life revolves around her sister. Entirely. She spends her mornings in Olathe taking Katie to speech therapy, then they visit a psychologist and then there's physical therapy. Stephanie reminds her sister to eat. She drives her around town. She tells her several times a day what is next on the schedule. Katie can't remember for herself.

"In a way I'm lucky," Katie says. "I don't remember any of it. It's like my short-term memory is gone. I see stuff on television, and it's almost like the whole thing happened to somebody else. Stephanie remembers everything for me."

The memory haunts Stephanie Dallam. Not just the aftermath,

when Katie Dallam lurched in and out of coherence following a one-day coma, when her eyes sunk deep into the sockets, her face was black, her body clung to a respirator, a blood clot weighed on her brain. Doctors said she might not survive. "That night," Stephanie Dallam says, "I kept waiting for the phone to ring (and for someone) to ask me if we wanted to donate the organs."

No, it goes beyond the coma, beyond the 3 1/2-hour surgery to repair a vein that had been torn at the top of the brain, beyond the broken nose and the hollow eyes, beyond the terrible moments at the bedside when she thought Katie was dead, beyond the terrible moments when she understood that Katie might survive but would never be the same.

It goes beyond the weeks in the hospital, beyond the brief time when Katie wanted to kill herself, beyond the daily grind of telling her sister the same stories again and again. Stephanie Dallam had been a critical-care nurse in Columbia. She had seen pain before. "I've seen hundreds of people die," she says. "It was agonizing watching Katie in pain."

No. The fight itself is what haunts Stephanie Dallam.

"A women's boxing match in rural Missouri is one step up from a dogfight," she says. "I'm not even sure it's one step up."

"Everybody knew they were supposed to be rooting for the other girl. She came in wearing the shorts; she was cuter, and so everybody screamed for blood. Katie was just an opponent. They just threw her in and let her get beat up. And they wouldn't stop it. It just kept going on and on, and the people were screaming, 'Kill her,' and nobody stopped it."

Stephanie Dallam is angry. Katie can't return to her job as a counselor. She can't drive, because she forgets where she's going. Small changes frighten her. She can't read, because it hurts her eyes. She can't jog, because it jars the brain. And often by the end of sentences, she forgets what she was saying. Doctors say it will take six more months to determine whether all the damage is permanent. They are not optimistic.

"We don't ever talk about the future," Stephanie says. "It upsets Katie too much. She had a master's degree. She was an athlete. She ran half-marathons. Now we have to deal with the fact that this might be Katie's life, and it's just too hard. We look one day ahead. We can't look beyond that."

Stephanie and Katie have hired an attorney, Sly James, and they are contemplating a lawsuit. James won't specify against whom. Meanwhile, Stephanie Dallam fights insurance companies. She fights with Social Security people. She takes care of her sister. The fight has changed Stephanie's life completely, too.

"These people ... they threw her in the ring and didn't protect her," she says. "I used to be naive. I used to believe that people would do the things they promised. They promised my sister everything would be all right."

Campbell explained, however, that both fighters had signed a customary disclaimer acknowledging the danger. No one, he added, promises safety in the ring.

"I hate what happened to Katie," Campbell says. "But there is risk in boxing like there is in all sports. You get hit in the head. Everybody who steps in the ring knows that."

Since Katie Dallam has left the hospital, she has longed to see a video of the fight. She wants to know what happened. She wants to see where everything went wrong. Stephanie vows to never see the tape.

"I saw the fight once," she says. "That was too much."

*   *   *

Sumya Anani is a contender. She has six victories and zero defeats now. She has knocked out two opponents since that night in December. Christy Martin's people have called for a fight. Others shy away. "Women are scared of her," her trainer, Barry Becker, says.

"I don't want to hear that tough-guy, male-dominated garbage," Anani says. "Nobody is afraid of me. That's the kind of stupid stuff you hear in male boxing. 'Oh, he's afraid.' That's so stupid. It makes me mad. I want women's boxing to be different than that."

Anani says she fights only to spread the word of the healing touch. She studies holistic healing. "I know that sounds kind of weird," Anani says. "But I know that's why I'm here. People always say, 'Why am I here?' I know. I'm here to tell people that life is in their health. People make themselves sick. I'm hear to spread the word that they don't have to live with the pain."

Anani did not hear about Katie Dallam's injury the night of the fight. When she heard the next day, she went to the hospital and held a candlelight vigil in the waiting room. She asked to give Dallam a healing massage in the intensive-care unit. She wrote a long letter to Dallam and asked her to move in. "We'll climb trees together and sing songs," she wrote.

"I'm sure they thought I was a quack," Anani says. "But I was a wreck. I kept writing and writing, and I'm no writer. I had my book on the healing touch with me. I just wanted to do something to help her."

The two have not seen each other since the fight. Katie Dallam says she does not blame Anani. These are the things that happen in the ring. But she has no desire to see her. Anani has not tried to make contact since that day in the hospital.

"I asked them to call me, and they never did," Anani says. "I feel bad. I considered quitting boxing. But I don't believe things just happen by accident. I think there's a reason this happened. I think someday we will connect again. I believe that."

For now, Anani works out three times a day. She says she's ready to fight anytime. She might have a fight sometime next month, though things change quickly in this game. She says the publicity after the Dallam fight has given her an opportunity to tell more people about the healing touch.

"Ironic, isn't it?" she says.

*   *   *

One day Katie Dallam painted the fight. She does not remember the fight. She does not remember the weeks leading up to the fight. She does not remember the weeks afterward. All of it is a blur, a nightmare forgotten. She knows only that she is not the same anymore. And that there was a fight.

"Sometimes, I think I remember things," she says. "But then, it's gone. I guess it's good I don't remember too much."

Talk comes hard. Before the fight, Dallam spoke breathlessly, crashing words together, but now she squints and pauses, struggling to find the simplest words. Each day she works with a speech therapist. Progress is slow.

So, without the words, she painted the fight. Details still hide behind her memory. She often painted before the accident — she was an art major at Missouri — though she usually concentrated on things like cactuses and people in her portraits. She painted for love in those days. This time she painted for anger.

"Sometimes, I think it's hard for Katie to express the rage of what happened to her," her sister says. "Sometimes, she still doesn't understand what happened to her."

Dallam painted an angry crowd that gazes down, a man with horns, deformed faces, faraway eyes. She painted a cage, and inside the cage is a big fighter throwing a hard jab. Inside the cage there is a little fighter, trying to cover up, only she cannot cover up, and a dark red spills from her head; it spills out into the cage, into the ring, and off the canvas.

Funny, she still likes boxing. She watches it when she can. She hopes the doctors let her work out again someday, though she never wants to step in the ring. No, she would just like to hit the heavy bag for a while.

"Boxing made me feel strong," Dallam says. "I had never felt strong before. I had always been afraid. I didn't want to be afraid anymore. I wanted to be strong. It made me feel so good.

"If I knew everything beforehand, I would not have fought. I thought it would be, like, a sport. I didn't think anybody would get hurt. I had seen women box before, and nobody got hurt. No woman had ever gotten hurt like me, I guess. I don't know what happened. I guess I'm bitter about it, but I don't know."

Katie Dallam looked down at her painting, the cage, the red, the howling faces. Stephanie asked her sister what she thought about when she painted it. Katie stared blankly.

"I don't remember," she said.

— **June 8, 1997**

PRODIGIES

Our JaRon Rush story begins, strangely enough, in a small church where a small boy plays some swinging jazz. His name is Eldar Djangirov, and he's 13, and his fingers tumble over the keyboard like raindrops in a storm. He's ripping through some Duke Ellington, and the music shakes the church. Who could know that such a small body could have so much soul?

Eldar's parents moved him to Kansas City from the old Soviet Union to get him close to the soul of jazz, to bring him up in the echoes of Charlie Parker and Count Basie and Jay McShann and the other geniuses who would play jazz beyond midnight on 18th and Vine. Eldar has played at the Grammy Awards and at Jazz Festivals everywhere. Already, in jazz circles across America, they whisper about Eldar Djangirov. The jazz prodigy.

So you ask, "What does this Eldar have to do with JaRon Rush?" Well, not so long ago, the whispers swirled around JaRon Rush. The basketball prodigy. And when you hear Eldar play this way, wide open, fingers running and scurrying, church quaking, people swaying in the pews, well, is it so different than seeing JaRon Rush pounding up the court, dribbling through his legs, zipping a pass to a teammate he could not have seen, the fans stomping on the wooden bleachers in delight?

What happens to the prodigies? Tiger Woods won all the major championships by the time he was 26. David Clyde pitched in a sold-out Texas stadium just days after graduating high school, but he never became a great pitcher. Jennifer Capriati's tennis career and life have flickered between greatness and chaos.

What will happen to Eldar Djangirov? Will he play Carnegie

Hall and record music that jolts America? Will he change music, the way Charlie Parker did? What will happen to him?

And what happened to JaRon Rush?

*   *   *

JaRon Rush was 14 years old the first time he shattered a backboard. Imagine all the other 14-year-olds out there, running at the basket, jumping as high as they could, stretching their fingers brushing the bottom of the net. And they would scream; Got the net!

There in that scene was Jaron, 6-feet-4 already. His fingers wrapped halfway around the basketball. His legs were like springs. He could dunk forward and backward and with feeling.

"Do a 360, JaRon," friends would plead, and sometimes he would, four hard steps, leaping, spinning, slamming. Ballet, man. That's what that was.

Only, that wasn't what caught your eye about JaRon Rush. It was the way he moved on the basketball court, smoothly, confidently, always in the right place, like a great boxer. He could score any time he wanted, of course, but he would rather pass, make someone else feel good for a moment. Where had he learned that? Kid had a lot of love.

JaRon had grown up playing basketball at a park, by the light of the street lamps. His mother wanted him home by 9:30, but the games would get hot and heavy, and JaRon could not leave. Glenda Rush would stand by the window and look out for her son. She could almost hear the cheers through the window.

"He just had this aura about him," said Kevin Pritchard, an old star at Kansas who would play in games with JaRon sometimes. "You couldn't believe he was that young. He just knew how to play the game. And it wasn't something anyone taught him. It came from his heart."

That's how it is for the prodigies. *Hoop Scoop*, a recruiting magazine, declared him the best young player in America when he was 15 years old. Oh, you could see his future greatness. And everyone around wanted to help JaRon Rush make it all the way.

There was Tom Grant, a millionaire who fell for JaRon when he was only 11, who wanted to give JaRon a chance. He paid for JaRon to go to Pembroke Hill. He helped him lease a car. He took him on vacation. There was nothing he wouldn't do for JaRon Rush. "We love him, and he's part of our family," Grant would say.

There was Myron Piggie, a streetwise coach with a shaky past, but a man who said he wanted to put all that behind him and help talented kids play basketball. He spent all his time working with those kids. "I love JaRon like a son," Piggie would say.

And there were all the high school coaches and college coaches and teachers and family members and recruiters, and they all loved Jaron, they all wanted to protect him, they all wanted to guide him. Jaron's first game at Pembroke, he was swarmed by kids who wanted his autograph. He still had braces on his teeth when UCLA coach Jim Harrick promised him a scholarship, and when Paul Mertens, a player at St. Mary's, said after a game, "It's kind of neat to say you played against a guy who'll be in the NBA someday."

There was so much love floating around JaRon. His brother Kareem was on his team. Everyone kept telling him how great he would be, how he would make millions of dollars and be on television. And it was about then, when JaRon Rush was 16, that he was asked about basketball. "It's gotten kind of boring," he said softly, "because I've played a lot of it."

Tom Grant never expected that people would think he did all those kindnesses for JaRon just to get him to go to Kansas. But that's exactly what people thought. Grant was a Kansas booster, right? JaRon was considering Kansas, right? Hey two-plus-two always equals four, right?

And so, recruiting was getting pretty hot, pretty dicey. The NCAA checked it out and cleared everyone, and that's about when Jim Harrick was fired, allegedly for lying, and then JaRon said he was worried about going to Kansas because he thought NBA scouts wouldn't see him enough. Then Kansas coach Roy Williams said he was no longer recruiting JaRon, and JaRon said he would go to UCLA, and in his last high school game in Kansas City, at Hickman Mills, JaRon Rush dunked so hard that the backboard shattered. Pembroke Hill paid $1,260 to replace it.

Soon after that, Rush left UCLA because he was homesick. He went back, and news came out that Myron Piggie had given him money while he was in high school. And the NCAA suspended Rush. And then, after playing just nine games his sophomore season, Rush declared himself eligible for the NBA draft. He was not drafted.

And so on. You can spend days following the money, chasing the allegations, but that's not what this story is about.

*   *   *

In the Penn Valley gymnasium two weeks ago, JaRon Rush was getting pushed around. He was 21 years old, the youngest man on the court, but he looked much, much younger. This was a Kansas City Knights practice — the new ABA team in town — and out there on the court, it was rough, rugged, vicious. You had Haywoode Workman, a longtime NBA player, and he was banging away, making plays. You had Rex Walters, that tough old Kansas guard with NBA experience, slamming through the lane. You had lots of guys playing for their lives.

And JaRon seemed to be trying to find his place, like someone's little brother who had run on the court. The brilliant talent, well, you could still see at times, the speed, the grace, the leaping ability, but mostly JaRon Rush was getting yelled at for cutting the wrong way, for not attacking the glass, for not moving right. Like his compass had busted.

"I think he got satisfied," said Kevin Pritchard, now the coach of the Kansas City Knights. "He did not keep working hard. Those gifts rust over if you don't work hard."

When practice ended, JaRon Rush talked about how he felt good about his life. True, the NBA had not given him a chance this time, but he's still young, still talented, and he felt certain that he could recapture the magic in Kansas City, his hometown.

"I'm exactly where I want to be," he said. "I've had a lot of things happen to me in my life, but I just know that I can play good basketball here. And people will notice."

Then, he walked out into a hallway, where three strangers were sitting on a bench. "Hey, you're somebody," one of them said. "What's your name?"

"JaRon."

"JaRon Rush?"

"Yeah."

And the three strangers looked very excited. But, they really didn't know what to say after that. They just smiled and waved to him. He waved back.

*   *   *

One week later, JaRon Rush was traded to the Los Angeles Stars.

Our JaRon Rush story ends, strangely enough, in a small

church where a small boy plays swinging jazz. Well, maybe the story goes on. People have their theories why JaRon Rush has not triumphed. Some say he didn't work hard enough. Some say he was let down by the people around him. Some say he got caught up in the glory, and he stopped playing from the heart, the way he played in the park, way past curfew, when he was 14.

Nobody really knows for sure, though. Did people use JaRon Rush? Maybe. But people helped him too, they cared for him, they loved him. Did JaRon Rush make mistakes? Sure he did, but were they big and bad enough to destroy his brilliant talent? There's wreckage now. Myron Piggie is in jail, and Tom Grant has moved on in his life, and it's Kareem Rush, JaRon's younger brother, who plays inspired and beautiful basketball at Missouri. He's the one the NBA scouts watch closely.

Meanwhile, JaRon Rush tries to rebuild his game and his life in a second-rate league far from where he grew up. He just might do it, too. That talent still roars inside him. He can do it, right? You want to believe. Because as that jazz prodigy Eldar Djangirov makes his piano bounce in that small church, you hear more than just sweet jazz. You hear the music of a young heart.

That's the music JaRon Rush played.

It's too soon for that music to be snuffed out. Isn't it?

— **Dec. 17, 2000**

SECRETARIAT: A LEGEND BLOOMS

PARIS, Ky. — There are always flowers on Secretariat's grave. Buck takes care of them. In winter, Buck sometimes takes the flowers in at night, sets them in warm water, brings them out again come morning. In summer, he brings by cold water, douses the flowers. Thursday, he left red carnations and the roses and day lilies in the Kentucky rain.

"Greatest thoroughbred who ever lived," Buck says. He's a groomsman at Claiborne Farms in Paris, Ky., that's in Bourbon County, and he doesn't have any deep thoughts about why America still has a love affair with Secretariat, who won the Triple Crown 25 years ago, who died nine years ago. He doesn't have a long explanation why flowers come every day, even now.

"Greatest thoroughbred who ever lived," Buck says again, and he shrugs, and that's that.

Secretariat means horse racing, the old stuff, when the game was still center stage, the sport of kings, much in the same way Ali means old boxing, and Foyt means the old Indy 500, and Mantle means baseball. People, especially old people, always say things were better in the old days. Well, they were better, at least in horse racing, when Secretariat ran.

"I've often wondered," says Cot Campbell, the owner of 1990 Preakness Winner Summer Squall, "if Secretariat is such a majestic name or it just sounds so majestic because he was such a grand horse. But that name is horse racing. It rolls off the tongue ... Secretariat."

Secretariat started last at the 1973 Kentucky Derby, 25 years ago. He started last and passed each horse, one by one, until the homestretch, when he passed a horse called Sham and won by two lengths in record time. He won the Preakness Stakes two weeks later. He then completed the Triple Crown, winning the Belmont Stakes by 31 lengths, perhaps the greatest run by a thoroughbred. By then, he was the most famous athlete in America, right there with Muhammad Ali and Pete Rose.

But unlike other horses who had their moments and then faded away, Secretariat began to stand for something. Other horses would win the Triple Crown. Seattle Slew would dominate 1977. Affirmed and Alydar would wage horse racing's greatest duel in 1978, with Affirmed winning each of the three races by smaller margins. There were other great horses, Sunday Silence, Alysheba, Cigar, Silver Charm.

They were not Secretariat. When he was alive, people — thousands of them, even people who did not care about horse racing — would drive to Kentucky to visit him. They would drive along the Kentucky Scenic Highway, ooh at the rolling hills of grass, white houses with columns, brick houses with spires on rooftops, horses grazing in the distance, all behind stone walls that were built 80 or 90 years before.

Yes, this was what they wanted to see, a simpler time, when horse racing mattered. Secretariat died in 1989, and the horse farms still line the road, there are signs to tell you how old the walls are ("Stone wall: Built in 1910"), and people still come by Claiborne Farm, just to see the tombstone, a plain thing, just to hear Buck explain how most horses are not buried whole, it's not practical, but they made a coffin for Secretariat because, well, he was the greatest racehorse who ever lived.

"Somehow, Secretariat just gets bigger and bigger every year," says Bob Baffert, trainer of the Kentucky Derby favorite Indian

Charlie.

Horse racing has lost so much of its charm, mostly because it's lousy on television. There's no way to capture the speed of the horses, their brute strength, the beauty of the thing. The sound of horses pounding down the backstretch is enormous, a medley of wind and hooves and snorts and whips cracking. On television, it sounds like an old Lash LaRue movie. Cloppity-clop. It sounds like the little mechanical horse out front of the supermarket that vibrates for a quarter. Brrrrr.

No, they can't make horse racing exciting on television — they can make pro wrestling exciting, though — so horse racing falls a little bit more each year. People will watch the Kentucky Derby on Saturday because it's the Kentucky Derby and all, and then most will ignore the sport again for another year. It's the way it goes.

But then, people keep sending flowers to Secretariat's grave day after day, perhaps to keep touch with a time gone by or perhaps to remember when they were young and horse racing mattered, perhaps, simply, as Buck says, because he was the greatest thoroughbred who ever lived.

— **May 1, 1998**

WHAT HAPPENED TO CLASS?

B eware, this is the fuddy-duddy column of all time, the "when I was your age I had to walk seven miles through the snow to school, uphill, both ways" column, the "back in my day people gave you an honest day's work" column.

This is the column about all the celebrations in the NFL.

"I know people will say, 'Aw, he's just an old player,' " says the greatest Chiefs receiver, Otis Taylor. "But I really, really don't like all this celebrating. It's all over the place. You've got big linemen dancing. You've got receivers going crazy around the goalpost. That looks absolutely stupid."

You're going to get a few old-timers saying those types of things in this column. But, then, wasn't it better when people just played the game? Aren't you tired of players gyrating after making routine plays, tired of watching running backs dance after 1-yard runs, tired of guys getting in guys' faces after simple tackles, tired of it all? Backup quarterbacks cha-cha when they send in the right signals these days. Trainers do backflips after wrapping an ankle correctly. Could you imagine the great moments in history if everybody acted like NFL players?

ROME — The great painter Michelangelo broke his clavicle in two places Tuesday after falling from the ceiling of the Sistine Chapel. Sources say he was trying to flex after painting the "Creation of Adam." He is listed as day-to-day.

LONDON — Many in the streets of London were surprised when famed playwright William Shakespeare walked up to fellow writer Sir Francis Bacon and slammed a copy of "King Lear" at his feet. Witnesses said Shakespeare then started pointing at Bacon and screaming, "In thine face, methinks."

PITTSBURGH — Jonas Salk admitted today that it will take at least two more weeks to release his polio vaccine for testing. "I got so excited after discovering the vaccine," Salk said, "that I spiked the test tube."

Marty Schottenheimer does not like all the celebrating and taunting that goes on in the NFL these days. You can bet on that. This league used to have men in it. Jim Brown who would drop the football in the end zone when he scored. Jim Taylor who would hand the ball to the referee. Merlin Olsen helped up quarterbacks. Men.

"It's like a parade now," Schottenheimer says wearily. "Everybody's doing some kind of dance or move."

He shakes his head. Schottenheimer is an old-time football guy, a mud-and-guts guy, an old linebacker who ran his heart out on special teams, and you can bet that all this celebrating and dancing and taunting and spiking and stuff makes him sick.

But, let's face it, he doesn't do much about it.

"You can't turn back the clock," he says, and he shakes his head. "You can't go back. It would be naive of me to think you could."

Ah, but Schottenheimer is already naive about so many things, isn't he? He works his players harder than virtually any other coach, so hard in fact that during the off-season, free-agent running back Robert Smith asked about it. Schottenheimer did not back off one bit ("We do work hard here," he confirmed, and Smith signed with Minnesota), and he has not backed off so many of his other principles. They say he's a stubborn man.

But his players juke and salute and flex and taunt, and Schottenheimer backs away. This week, even Tony Richardson, as classy and hard-working a player as any on the Chiefs, spiked the ball in a punter's face after recovering a blocked punt. Richardson said he got excited, he did not know the punter was there, blah blah blah, but are those really reasons?

"Look, you don't want to take away the players' enthusiasm," Schottenheimer says, and he proceeds to talk about how even the understated and classy Bill Mazeroski pumped his fist after hitting the game-winning home run in the 1960 World Series.

Yeah, tell you what, Marty, when one of your guys wins a Super Bowl with a dazzling 85-yard run, he can dance to his heart's content. In the meantime, it sure would be nice to see an old-time coach step up and stop the dancing.

*   *   *

Let's see if we can keep up: Atlanta players do the Dirty Bird, and the New Orleans guys play leapfrog, and Carolina's Fred Lane does some sort of worm dance, and Andre Rison unveils a Spider-Man move, and Jacksonville's Keenan McCardell re-enacts famous basketball moves, and San Francisco's Merton Hanks does that weird neck thing, and Dallas' Deion Sanders does his own Deion dance, and Neil Smith swings his baseball swing, and the other Broncos salute, and Packers jump in the stands, and wait, there are others.

"Maybe they should bring those guys before the game, have them pose and dance and do all that nonsense," says Roman Gabriel, a longtime NFL quarterback. "Then, you award a point or two for whoever does it best, and get on with the game."

Yes, this is the segment where the old-timers speak. Marcus Allen tells a story about how, when he was with the Chiefs, players used to walk up to his locker and ask about some new move or dance they planned to use for the next touchdown. Allen, who never did anything after a touchdown but run off the field, just shook his head.

"I used to high-step sometimes," says Taylor, who scored 60 touchdowns, more than any other Chiefs player ever. "But that was it. I did not dance or sing or slam the ball in a guy's face. I always thought that when a receiver does that, a cornerback should be into them right then and there. You don't embarrass other players. They've got kids watching the game, too. It's not right."

Yes, player after player talks about how he doesn't like this stuff. But who stops it? Coaches? Few seem willing to take on something like this. Fans? No way, this stuff will keep getting on "SportsCenter," and we will keep on watching. The NFL? Well, for a while, the NFL did try to stop the celebrating, and that didn't work too well. People said the NFL stood for "No Fun League," and players complained they couldn't express themselves (to which you might say "Hey, you want to express yourself, write poetry"), and fans said the games became stale, unemotional.

Truth is, you can't legislate class. Maybe the NFL, like soccer, could come up with a yellow-card and red-card system; you taunt once you get the yellow, you taunt again and you're out of the game. Or, maybe there should be a two-minute penalty for players who prance, so their team for two minutes has to play short-handed, 10

T H E   G O O D   S T U F F

men against 11. Hey, you think you're bigger than the team, why
don't you just go into that penalty box and we'll find out?

Or maybe players should be allowed to dance if they want, but
afterward the other team gets one free shot at them.

Or, maybe, one day, the players will run out of dances and ways
to spike the ball, they will be all out of salutes and shuffles and dirty
birds, and they will go back to playing football, blocking, tackling,
running, catching, the real football stuff, and then celebrating as
much as they want after actually winning the game.

"Sure, I played in a time when you celebrated after victories,"
Gabriel says. "Funny, we thought that was the way you were
supposed to do it."

— **Dec. 18, 1998**

TIGER SHOWS HIS HEART

L OUISVILLE, Ky. — Tiger Woods showed us his heart out there.
He had never shown us that before — not really. He had shown
us power and grace and smiles and scowls and that supercool
television commercial trick where he bounced a golf ball in the air
over and over to the beat of jazzy music.

He was a phenomenon. A superstar. A comic-book hero? Did we
know Tiger Woods? Not really. He won golf tournaments so
effortlessly, so easily, that he hardly seemed human. He was
Superman. He flew in, saved the day and flew away.

Sunday, though, at the PGA Championship, we got to know
Tiger Woods. He faced off against the most unlikely of rivals, a 5-
foot-7 golfer with preposterous daring and the plainest of names,

Bob May. No matter what Tiger Woods did, Bob May would not back down. He matched Woods putt for putt, brilliant shot for brilliant shot, on and on, until it was so tense and wonderful that it was almost unbearable.

And, finally, Tiger Woods' will burst through.

He won on the 21st hole of the day, the third playoff hole, with a 1-foot putt that dropped softly into the center of the cup. He pumped his fist.

Then he hugged Bob May.

"We never backed off from one another," Woods said. "And birdie for birdie, shot for shot, we were going right at each other. That was just so much fun. That's as good as it gets right there."

First, there is golf history to sum up. Woods became the first man to win back-to-back PGA Championships in 63 years. Even more, he became the first golfer to win three major championships in one year since Ben Hogan did it in 1953.

Woods did that in grand style. First, in June, he won the U.S. Open at Pebble Beach by an unprecedented 15 shots. Then, in July, he won the British Open at the birthplace of golf, St. Andrews in Scotland, with the lowest score in major championship history.

Then came Louisville. The golf course, Valhalla, has no grand tradition to speak of, no particular beauty, and it may have been the easiest golf course ever played in major championship golf. On Saturday alone, 53 players shot under par. On Sunday most expected Tiger Woods to simply destroy the field in a colorless, drab sort of way.

"He hits the ball farther than anybody," Kansas City's Tom Watson said of Woods. "He putts better than anybody. He chips better than anybody. He wants to be the best player who ever lived .... It's going to be tough for anyone to beat him."

Instead, this character, Bob May, son of a gas station owner, emerged. You could not have found a more unlikely foil. May had been a fine junior golfer in California — 20 minutes from Tiger Woods' home, in fact — but then his game abandoned him. He went to Europe to find it and played there for four years.

He returned to the United States earlier this year. When he was invited to play in the PGA Championship, many golfers were surprised. Truth is, he had not played particularly well.

But Sunday, May was ferocious. Woods had grown used to intimidating other golfers. He won the U.S. Open by 15 shots; he won the British Open by eight shots. Three years ago he won the other major championship, the Masters, by 12 shots. All the talk this week was how nobody was good enough to challenge him.

"We're trying," said Europe's best golfer, Colin Montgomerie. "We're failing. But we're trying."

So nobody is sure how this fellow, Bob May, did it. But no matter how great a shot Woods hit, May hit one better. Through 16 holes, May had a one-shot lead. And it was May who looked invincible and Woods who suddenly looked vulnerable.

"You have to reach deep inside yourself," Woods said. This had been the only question. Could he reach inside? He rarely had to. He was so good that even Jack Nicklaus, the greatest golfer of them all, found it hard to find the words to describe Woods.

"What can I say?" he asked. "Think of all the words for great. String them together."

On the 17th hole, Woods hit his drive 324 yards down the heart. Nobody in the world could do that. Nobody in the history of the world could do that. Then Woods hit his shot to within 2 feet. He made the putt. He tied Bob May. Reach deep inside? He was only beginning.

"It was really something," May would say.

The cheers, the sun, the humidity, the pressure, all of it, and these two guys were not playing on talent anymore. They were playing on sheer will. They say that boxers, in the late rounds, get to a point where they are so exhausted, they don't even know what's keeping them going. That's the place Woods and May had reached.

"You just had to keep making birdies," Woods said.

On the 18th, May made his birdie with a ludicrous downhill putt that was a bit like trying to putt a ball down a car windshield into a Dixie Cup. Woods then made his birdie with a shorter, but equally trying, putt as everyone in Louisville held their breath.

"Can you imagine," a fan said as Woods pumped his fist, "what it must be like to be him?"

They were still tied, and that meant three extra holes. Woods took the lead with a 20-foot-putt. He followed and stalked the ball all the way to the hole.

"Get in," he screamed. And it did. Woods led by a shot.

And then the last two holes were wild. Woods hit the ball into a gully, then near a water drain; May hit his into two sand traps. Woods hit the ball onto a cart path; May hit his way too close to water. They had nothing left to give. But somehow they kept going. On the last hole, Woods was in the sand.

"Well," he told himself, "hit it close."

He hit the ball to within a foot of the hole. When May missed his putt, Woods knew. He had won. And this had been different from all the other victories. He had set all sorts of records. But this one had been all heart.

"I think it's got to go down as one of the best duels in the history of the game," Woods said.

Early in the week, someone had asked him whether he would

rather win by 20 — you know, blow away the competition — or get into a back-and-forth, rock 'em-sock 'em duel to the finish. Woods had said he would rather win by 20. Life's a lot easier that way.

But life's a lot more fun this way.

— Aug. 21, 2000

OOF!

Before I tell you what it's like to get hit in the side with a soccer ball moving 70 mph, let me say that this participatory journalism jazz has got to stop. You sit in a hockey penalty box once, on a lark, and next thing you know you're fumbling through two hours of radio, and then suddenly grown men are whacking soccer balls at your head.

Then editors are asking for these stories:

1. What it feels like to get hit with a major-league fastball.

2. The wall at Indy and the agony of being on fire.

3. Hockey helmets, do they really work?

4. Sounds you make after getting hit by Mike Tyson's uppercut.

5. Pro wrestling: real or fake? (A firsthand account).

So we're going to stop right here because you should have seen the gleam in the eyes of those Attack players as they cranked shots at me. These are men who have been hit with soccer balls all their lives, men who have taken the bullet again and again to prevent goals in arenas and cities across America, and their backs hurt, and their knees throb, bruises everywhere, and a lady in the third row called them bums, and suddenly they had a chunky, balding, smart-aleck columnist in goal.

The ball at their feet.

A nice letter to the editor would have been better.

*   *   *

Blair Quinn, who got cut from the team Thursday, explained goalkeeping best. Before any of this madness began, back when I had full use of my right arm, I asked him the first question of goalkeeping in indoor soccer: How the heck do you get out of the way?

"You can't," he said. "If the ball's going to hit you, the ball's going to hit you. Nothing you can do about it."

Understand, there isn't much of anything you can do as an indoor soccer goalie. Sure, it takes gifts, quickness, good hands, fast reactions, all that, but this isn't like the outdoor game where goalkeepers play position, near post, far post, where they have space to roam. No, in the indoor game you have one stinking job, and that's to somehow get your body in front of the ball.

Players make it easy.

"OK, guys, aim for the goalkeeper's head," Attack coach Jim Schwab screamed. "Hit the guy's head. Knock it off."

"How does that make you feel?" I asked Kevin Zimmerman, a 22-year-old still figuring out this indoor soccer thing.

"Oh that doesn't bother me," he says. "It's hard to hit somebody's head."

These are the words that comforted me.

*   *   *

Soccer balls can do amazing things in the air. One guy — think it was Kevin Koetters, though who can follow the game at this speed? — kicked a smokin' ball that headed right toward my neck.

Obviously, this created a bit of concern (the usual stuff, lightheadedness, nausea, the central nervous system screaming DANGER, WILL ROBINSON), but suddenly the ball swerved left, switched lanes, swooped upward and — this may have been an illusion — started laughing.

"Looked like the ball caught an air pocket on you," Zimmerman said.

"Hate when those balls catch air pockets," injured goalie Warren Westcoat said.

Great. It's not bad enough that soccer balls splatter against your body, making you feel like a car windshield riding along on the highway — you also have to worry about air pockets. What is this, TWA? Also the wall. The wall is a big part of indoor soccer, mainly because balls deflect off the walls, and it sounds like Dunkirk, and you as goalie are stuck in some giant pinball machine.

"Block the ball," assistant coach Gino Schiraldi screamed at me, excellent advice from an indoor soccer legend who got the heck out of the game and started making doughnuts and pizzas.

The first ball hit me in the shoulder. The second one in the side. That one hurt pretty good. One hit me in the back. Don't ask how that happened. The funny part is every time a ball hit me, everybody cheered. "You did good," Schiraldi screamed.

See, this is the job of the goalie. All your life, from days of dodgeball and kickball and driver's ed, you teach yourself to get the heck out of the way. It's strange to hear people cheer you for getting smacked with a soccer ball.

Special thanks: to defender Eddie Carmean, who dived in front of a ball and got hit in an area where, let's just say, men feel real pain. "He saved you," Schwab screamed, and indeed I — and also my children, years from now — will forever be grateful to Eddie

Carmean.

All of which leads to my single greatest achievement in indoor soccer. Three players bounced the ball around, back and forth, and suddenly there was a player wide open on the right, and the ball bounced to him, and I ran toward him, and he kicked some sort of Mack truck at me, which hit my chest, knocking my heart into the third row, collapsing my lungs and leaving a soccer ball imprint for all eternity.

"Great save," Zimmerman said, and Westcoat too, and they smacked me on the back, though that might have been to get me breathing again.

After that, Schwab let me play in the scrimmage as a midfielder, which mainly involves running around like an idiot. Indoor soccer players run constantly, not unlike Forrest Gump, and so it goes that Eloy Salgado, my favorite defender, ran around and screamed "The Chiefs are wimps."

Anyway, you run, and you run, and you run, and you run, and they call this a sport. I did get a shot on goal, from the top of the key, a glorious moment that was diminished somewhat when Schwab immediately stopped practice, pointed at Zimmerman and said, "If Joe scores, you're cut."

Also, Nate Houser kicked a ball that crashed into my back. Even out there you get hit with the ball. Everybody cheered again when the ball hit me because I had made such a great play. OK, maybe they were just thrilled to see me get hit really, really hard by the ball. Next time, I do one of these participation stories, it's going to be bowling, I promise.

— **Dec. 12, 1997**

HER MOMENT LOST

SYDNEY — Here was the saddest scene of these Olympic Games. A makeshift medal stand. Two Indonesian women standing on each side. A blank space at the top. A tiny United States flag on a tiny flagpole. A bland recording of a trumpet. No national anthem. No one around to watch.

This was the International Olympic Committee's gift to Tara Nott for playing fair.

This was her ceremony for winning a gold medal.

Sometimes in sports you see something so wrong, so unfair, so bleepin' sinful that you just want to find the moron in charge and slug him. Here was one of those moments. Tara Nott of Stilwell, Kan., became the first American to win a weightlifting gold medal in 40 years. Forty years.

But it's more than that. She won it by playing the game by the rules. Weightlifting at these Olympics has been an utter fiasco. The entire Bulgarian team was tossed out for failed drug tests. Several Romanians also got the boot.

And, in one of the most bizarre stories in Olympic history, Qatar hired a bunch of mercenaries from other countries, sort of like a weightlifting version of the Washington Redskins. Then, Qatar pulled out under mysterious circumstances. The official reason for the Qatar evacuation: Diarrhea. Now, those are mysterious circumstances.

Then you have Tara Nott, playing by the rules, giving up the other parts of her life so she could train. She left her Kansas home with no job, no friends, no apartment, just this crazy dream, and went to Colorado Springs, Colo., to prepare for these Games.

Olympic spirit? She cries madly just watching other people get medals.

Last Sunday, she won the silver medal. It was an amazing achievement. She had only been weightlifting for five years. She cried intensely, then she could not stop laughing, and up on the medal stand, she had one thought, one deep, penetrating thought, and it went like this: "WOW!"

"Goodness," she says now. "I can't even put it into words."

Tara Nott is one of just 23 people on planet Earth who actually use the word "Goodness!"

She was thrilled with her silver medal. She walked around Sydney with it, and people would come right up and ask to have their photo taken with her and the medal. Children would rush up to her, try to touch it. She would wrap the medal around their necks. What a feeling. There was her dad, Terry, who works in the post office, and her mom, Nada, and they were wandering around Australia with a silver medal. What a feeling.

Then, Thursday, Nott's cell phone rang. She had been wandering Darling Harbor. The voice on the other end asked whether this was Tara Nott.

"Yes, it is," Nott said.

"Is this Tara Nott the weightlifter?"

"Yes, it is."

"Is this Tara Nott the Olympic champion?"

She froze. A billion thoughts popped at once. It turned out that Bulgaria's Izabela Dragneva, who had lifted more weight than Nott, had tested positive for furosemide, a diuretic that helps lifters lose weight so they can make their weight class and can be used to help mask other drugs. Dragneva was stripped of her gold. Nott was now the gold medalist.

"I started jumping up and down," Nott said. "I couldn't believe it."

They went to a family barbecue, Nott and her boyfriend Kevin O'Conner, and there he suddenly called everyone's attention.

"A toast," he said, "to Tara. The Olympic champion."

And with that, everyone was jumping up and down, Mom and Dad, relatives and friends galore. Tears and laughter all over again.

And right there, it did not bother them how much they had been cheated. Nott deserved to win that gold medal during the event. Nott had to make weight, too, just like Dragneva. She ate chicken for weeks. She wore sweats into the sauna. She whittled off 10 pounds the way real champions do.

Yes, she deserved to win that gold in front of the big crowd. But there was no bitterness. Justice was served. The cheater was dismissed. Nott would get her gold-medal moment.

And that's when the IOC, that pathetic collection of letters, got involved. They announced there would be a small and meaningless ceremony in the athletes village. They told Nott it would be at 4 p.m. They said she could not have a real ceremony at the weightlifting site. They said all of this was non-negotiable.

It was outrageous. First, Nott could not make it at 4 p.m. Her teammate and friend Cheryl Hayworth was lifting at that time, and she wanted to be there to cheer for her. Plus her family could not make it. But more than anything, it wasn't right. Nott had earned a gold medal. She deserved a proper ceremony, with her family and a crowd and a big U.S. flag and the national anthem roaring. She deserved that.

But these IOC people — these vile, shortsighted, wretched IOC people — went on with their plan of having a makeshift medal ceremony where nobody could watch. This plan, apparently, went all the way to the top, to Juan Antonio Samaranch himself. Nott did not show up for the miserable ceremony. It went on, disgustingly, without her.

"In my opinion," said Dennis Snethen, the vice-president elect for U.S. Weightlifting, "they don't want another award assembly. They don't want to bring any more negative attention to weightlifting."

And that's where the IOC stooges got it wrong. Negative attention? This was a chance to show the world that maybe you can't catch every cheater, no, but you can catch some of them. This was a chance to stand up and say, "We'll have as many medal ceremonies as necessary until we get a winner worthy of a gold medal."

This was a chance to prove that weightlifting isn't always about diarrhea and drugs and mockeries — sometimes it's about real, live heroes.

This was a chance to wrap a medal around Tara Nott's neck and watch the tears roll down her face, those tears that come from someone who sacrificed her life, her job, her future for this moment. These Games are filled with so much doubt. Drug suspicions fly everywhere. A swimmer drops a couple of seconds off a personal-best time, and the whispers rush. A weightlifter lifts too many pounds, and people shake their heads.

This was the IOC's chance to save themselves. And they blew it. Whiffed. Tara Nott will have her ceremony. The U.S. Olympic Committee will put it on. Eventually, back home in Kansas, there will be a real celebration, a party for this woman who won a gold medal, who proved that she's the best in the world, who proved you can become the best with class and dignity and grace.

What a party there will be in Kansas.

And those IOC stooges are not invited. You know that blank

space on top of the medal stand, the one where Tara Nott was supposed to stand? You can see another one just like it, right where the IOC's heart is supposed to be.

— **Sept. 23, 2000**

NUMBER 23

There's nothing left to feel today. All the tributes have been written. All the beautiful words have been spoken. Michael Jordan has been called the greatest basketball player who ever lived so many times, by so many different people, that it has become a part of his name, an honorary title even, like Sir Laurence Olivier or Marvelous Marvin Hagler.

So, what's left? Once you've called Jordan the greatest, once you've reviewed his six championships, his 31.5 points-per-game average, his six playoff MVP awards, his five regular-season MVP awards, his two gold medals, his countless last-minute jump shots, his Nike commercials, his friendship with Bugs Bunny, his attempt to play baseball, his re-creation of the dunk, his billion trick shots, his elevating the NBA to the world stage and his recent selection in one poll as the greatest living hero (finishing ahead of, among others, Desmond Tutu and Jimmy Carter), once you've done all that, what's left?

All I can tell you is a personal story.

All I can tell you is how this man marked my life.

CHARLOTTE, N.C., 1982 — We were both young in North Carolina, where basketball is religion. My first day in high school, a big kid had asked me to name my favorite ACC team. I was a Cleveland kid, born and raised, and found that I could not name any ACC team, much less my favorite.

"North Carolina?" I guessed.

"Figures," the big kid said. "I'm an ABC fan."

"ABC?"

"Anyone but Carolina."

It was a March evening, then, and by then I had truly fallen for that North Carolina team, the grace of James Worthy, the half-hook of Sam Perkins, the fake jump shot of Matt Doherty, and of course, there was the kid, a freshman, Jordan, who could jump a mile high, and with seconds left, he made the jump shot, the one that beat Georgetown, the shot that first placed him in the stratosphere. Outside, car horns blared. Inside, I jumped up and down on the couch, over and over and over, until the phone rang.

"Congratulations," the big kid said.

CHARLOTTE, 1984 — The first time we met was on a cool spring night when Jordan was in town for a college all-star game. He was famous then, but not *famous*, not a major celebrity, surely not yet the most recognizable man in the world. He had hair. Barely 8,000 people watched him play that night. He dunked from the free-throw line for us.

And after the game, he walked slowly to his car, and a handful of us walked with him, tried to talk to him, mostly lunged for his autograph. He signed as he walked, and soon there was only one high school kid left. Jordan reached for a crumpled *Sports Illustrated* to sign, when suddenly, from a distance, someone yelled, "A-A-A-A! MICHAEL JORDAN!"

What followed was one of those scenes from the Beatles movies, where hundreds of shrieking teen-agers chased after John and Paul (and, especially Ringo), only this time they were after Jordan. His eyes opened wide. He ducked into his car, started the engine, opened the window and said the first words he would say to me: "Sorry, kid," he said. "I've got to go."

CLEVELAND, 1988 — Every single day we argued about the best player in the NBA. Heck, we were in college. What else was there to argue about other than Miller vs. Budweiser? We argued NBA fiercely, and there was the Larry Bird camp, the Magic Johnson camp (which I was in) and the rapidly growing Michael Jordan camp. We used to scoff at the Jordanettes.

"All he does is dunk," we used to say. "Take away his breakaway dunks, and he's a mediocre player."

Oh, how the arguments raged. Then, we were gathered in a sports bar on a Sunday, watching Cleveland beat Chicago in a playoff game, and we were laughing in the faces of the Jordanettes — mocking them — when there were 3 seconds on the clock, and everybody knew Jordan would get the ball. He got it. He dribbled left, jumped. Cleveland's Craig Ehlo jumped with him. Jordan lingered in the air longer, longer, then shot the jump shot as he faded to the left. He hit it.

And he jumped in the air and pumped his fist again and again and again.

Oh, how the Jordanettes sang.

AUGUSTA, Ga., 1992 — One week a year, all is golden in Augusta. The people who run the Masters must have a pipeline to the heavens, because that week the flowers bloom, and humidity goes on vacation, and the restaurants (bless their money-grubbing hearts) actually stay open past 8 p.m.

No words can describe life there in June, though, when temperatures rise into the high 90s, and humidity descends like a biblical plague, and opening the front door is like opening the portal to the fire compartment on an old coal train. We sat around there, five miserable young guys, all with big dreams, all with small apartments, we sat around and watched a fuzzy 19-inch television, watched as Michael Jordan made a three-pointer, and another, and another, and another, until finally he could only look at the sidelines, shrug his shoulders, as if to say "Man, I'm good."

"What would you give," Andy asked, "just to be him for a day?"

GREENVILLE, S.C., 1994 — They set up a picnic table in the bullpen, lined a few metal chairs around, and after an hour, Michael Jordan sat down.

"Why are you doing this?" we asked.

"This makes me happy," he said.

He had given up basketball. He had given up flying. He had given up dunking. He traveled from hot Southern town to hot Southern town, where he swung feebly at minor-league curveballs. He said he was chasing a childhood dream. It was hard to believe that a man who had already won three NBA championships, a man who scored 32 points a game, a man already regarded as the best who ever lived, it was hard to believe that he could find what he was looking for in these little stadiums, in front of a few thousand people, playing a sport that he could never conquer.

Then Jordan was looking, well, he was looking right at me.

"Let me ask you," he said. "Haven't you ever followed a dream?"

INDIANAPOLIS, 1995 — He looked slow. He looked skinny. He looked out of place. Everyone who had come to Market Square Arena had come to see Michael Jordan return, but instead, we were watching a different man, an old minor-league baseball player wearing No. 45. "He'll never be the same," the cigar-chomping man to the left said as we watched Jordan's jump shot plink off the rim.

"Why do you say that?"

"His time's past. It happens to all of them."

Jordan did, indeed, seem old. And if he was old, of course, that meant I was old, my friends too, all of us.

"You're crazy," I told the man. "He's back."

CHICAGO, 1997 — There was a buzz in the place. It had nothing to do with how well Michael Jordan played, it never had anything to do with that. No, with Jordan playing, there was just this sense that you were in exactly the right place, exactly the right time. You were at the center of the world.

Jordan, like Joe DiMaggio, used to say that he always wanted to play hard, with everything inside, because there might be a kid up in the rafters who had never seen him play before. So, he always did play hard, Sacramento to Miami, Madison Square Garden to McNichols Arena, he put on a show, every night.

Who knows how many he scored that night? Thirty? Forty? He had a few dunks. He made a couple of steals. He was no longer the phenomenon he was at 18, when he could jump over the rim, nor the scoring machine he was at 25 when his first step was lightning, and he dunked thunder.

No, he had found this fadeaway jump shot, unstoppable as mountain rain, and he had this presence about him, this iron will, he had won another championship, was now leading what is probably the greatest team in NBA history.

He had reached the highest level of all.

He acted as if the game were played by marionettes, and he pulled the strings.

We watched in wonder.

BANFF, Alberta, 1998 — We had cut our deal on this honeymoon. We would explore the world by day. But at night, we both wanted to see Michael Jordan. We wandered through some of the most beautiful places in the world, snow-capped mountains, crystal lakes. Elk wandered up to us as if they wanted a light.

In the evening, we watched Jordan on our tiny hotel television, watched him shoot that fadeaway jump shot over the Utah Jazz again and again, willing his team, dominating the screen, playing as only he had ever played.

"You know," I said, "this is it for him."

"Yeah," she said, "you're probably right."

We watched, and tried to freeze his image in our minds. Someday, a child, a son or niece or grandchild, will wander up, sit on the lap, ask what it was like to watch Michael Jordan play basketball, and I don't know what words will fit the question.

By then, there will probably be some Robo-Jordan, some guy jumping 8 feet in the air, dunking with his teeth, doing backflips over defenders, averaging 66 points a game.

"The greatest who ever lived," I will say.

"You're nuts," the precious little one will say, and I will begin to tell all about the shots and the dunks and the fadeaways and the steals and the tongue dangling and the crossover dribbles and the double-clutches and the celebrations, and probably decide that there's simply too much to say.

"You should have been there," I will say instead.

— Jan. 14, 1999

WHO STRIKES FEAR? ELWAY

MIAMI — In so many ways, of course, I'm absolutely the wrong person to write this appreciation of John Elway. I have never enjoyed watching Elway, never marveled at his arm strength, never delighted in seeing him tear away from tacklers, never thrilled at his bringing a team back from the abyss.

No, I don't like Elway, never have, not after he twice ripped apart my childhood love, the Cleveland Browns, not after he sent Kansas City into a yearlong depression with his late-game antics. While fans across America went all weepy two weeks ago, when Elway played what figures to be his last game at Mile High, I kept reading his eyes, studying his face, just to make sure that son-of-a-gun wouldn't change his mind about retiring.

Then, perhaps that makes me just the right guy to toast John Elway here as he enters what figures to be his last game, Sunday's Super Bowl, because truly, his career has not been about pretty passes or sweet runs or gaudy numbers. His greatness doesn't sprout from his touchdown runs or the way he could whip a ball 80 yards through the wind or even his ability, in the final minutes, to rally the Denver Broncos from behind in the fourth quarter.

"John Elway?" the great Oakland Raiders defensive lineman Howie Long says. "Let me tell you about John Elway. He was the biggest pain in the neck I ever played against. I'm serious. That guy was a nightmare."

So, ladies and gentlemen, raise your glasses to John Elway: The biggest pain in the neck who ever played professional football.

*   *   *

Nobody has ever frightened a defense quite like John Elway. That's his legacy. His quarterback rating — the mysterious number the NFL computes to consider quarterbacks — is a rather modest 79.9, placing him in the lagoon with men like Scott Mitchell and Jeff George. Ten years into his career, all of those for arch-conservative coach Dan Reeves, he had thrown 159 touchdown passes and 158 interceptions, hardly the stuff of legend.

But, always, even in the lean years, he launched terror in defenders and opposing fans because no quarterback who ever played the game could beat you so many different ways. Yes, Johnny Unitas could beat you with his will, and Roger Staubach with his shotgun arm, and Joe Montana with his assortment of cotton-candy passes. Long remembers once Joe Montana beat his Raiders 45-3, but he says: "It was like he hardly touched us. He just tossed a soft pass there, a dink here, you hardly felt it. Elway would rip your heart out."

Elway could run around anyone. He could throw a lightning bolt between two defenders. He could drag tacklers 5 or 6 yards to pick up a first down. He could unleash a football deep. For three quarters, he often stumbled around, threw interceptions, got crunched from behind. It was a setup. In the fourth, when it mattered, he simply could not be stopped.

"He gets that look in his eye, that look that says, 'I don't care what I have to do, we're going to win,' " Kansas City's new coach, Gunther Cunningham says. "That's what always impressed me about John. With some quarterbacks, you look in their eyes, you see fear. Never with John. He never blinks."

Over the years, Elway has brought the Broncos back in the fourth quarter 47 times, more than any other player ever. Those comebacks are what makes him so beloved in Denver. He's always the guy on the white horse. "He's like El Cid," Long says. "He's all banged up, beaten up, but you prop him up on the horse, and people run scared."

Elway's rookie season, when he was still a raw kid who had no idea what was going on, the Broncos trailed Baltimore 19-0. In the fourth quarter, Elway threw three touchdown passes in front of an entranced Denver crowd. The love affair began. Now, you can't go anywhere in Denver — anywhere — without seeing a photo of Elway.

"Think of New York, you think of the Empire State building," Denver tight end Shannon Sharpe says. "Think of San Francisco, you think of the Golden Gate Bridge and the TransAmerica Building. Think of Kansas City, you think of, oh, I don't know, cows maybe. Think of Denver, and you think of John Elway. That's all. John Elway."

*　　　*　　　*

Here's what it felt like for a Cleveland fan to watch John Elway drive his Broncos 98 yards down the field against the Browns in 1987: It really stunk. These days, it is one of the most famous drives in NFL history, the singular masterpiece of Elway's career, but that January afternoon, in the AFC championship game, it just plain stunk.

Elway did not know then that he had this sort of thing inside. He had been a pretty good quarterback but nothing overwhelming, certainly not the phenom everyone thought he would be when he was selected No. 1 in the NFL draft. When the Broncos got the football at the 2, and the Browns led by a touchdown, and the clock showed 5 minutes remaining, and 80,000 Cleveland fans unleashed all their years of frustration by screaming, well, Elway did not have any premonition of what he was about to do.

"I didn't feel all that good," he says now. He was 26 years old, facing a frigid wind and an angry crowd and a pretty good defense, and he did not know yet. He did not know yet that he was John Elway. Keith Bishop, a Broncos offensive guard, looked up at Elway and said, "Well, we've got them just where we want them."

Elway laughed.

And the rest, as they say, is agony. Elway dived for a first down. On third and 18, he hit a pass for 25. The Broncos kept moving. On the sidelines, a young coach, Marty Schottenheimer, just watched and watched, and at some point even he knew.

"John Elway," Schottenheimer says, "was going to find a way to beat us that day. It didn't matter what we did. He was going to find a way. He's the greatest competitor I've ever seen in any sport."

Elway completed the touchdown pass with 39 seconds left in the game.

"I have never thrown a football as hard as I threw that pass," he would say later.

*   *   *

John Elway, like Nolan Ryan, became truly magnificent when he no longer had those supreme skills, the stuff of gods. As a young player, with that limitless arm and breathtaking speed, he was wild, unbridled. He was, as Terry Bradshaw said at the time, a great talent but little more.

After Mike Shanahan arrived, after the Broncos drafted running back Terrell Davis, Elway no longer was asked to save the Broncos in the fourth quarter. He was asked to pitch the ball to Davis, throw more touchdown passes, take fewer chances and, mostly, lead.

"I would not be the player I am or the man I am without John Elway," Terrell Davis says. "I am in that huddle and John says, 'This is you, Terrell,' and all I can think is 'Don't let that man down.'"

Elway did not play all that well in last year's Super Bowl. He threw for 123 measly yards. His interception nearly cost the Broncos the game. But again, in the fourth quarter, he found a way, getting a big first down, diving headfirst for a touchdown, coaxing victory from his teammates.

In the AFC championship this year, he was absolutely miserable, barely completing a third of his passes, but again, when the game mattered, Elway hit, the Broncos won. Elway, as Cunningham says, does not blink.

"He's a better quarterback than I was, I have no problem saying that now," Bradshaw says now. "People change. John has changed. He's one of the all-time best."

Indeed, this is the last topic. Teammates and coaches believe Elway will not play again after Sunday. There are just too many aches and sprains and twinges to overcome anymore. So, what's left is to ask just where Elway belongs on sports history's ledger. The famous question goes: "Who would you want as your quarterback if you had to win the big game?" Plenty say Elway. Plenty others say Montana, who has won four Super Bowls, or Bradshaw or Unitas. Steve Sabol, president of NFL Films, picks the great Otto Graham, who took the Cleveland Browns to the NFL championship game every single year he was quarterback.

Personally, though, I think it's the wrong question.

No, the question should go like this: "If your beloved team was barely ahead in the fourth quarter, and the wind was howling, and the crowd was roaring, and you had all this hope inside, who would be the one quarterback that would strike fear into you, the one quarterback who you know would find a way to steal the game from you and send you into a spiraling depression?"

To that bitter question, there's only one answer.

— **Jan. 29, 1999**

ALL OR NOTHING AT ALL

Some years ago, after getting dumped hard, I slumped on the couch and played Sinatra through morning.

There's nothing in this world quite like listening to Frank Sinatra in the darkness after getting your heart squashed, nothing quite like hearing Sinatra croon "One for My Baby" so many times that each word beats at your chest. I never felt more dead.

Then there was this other time, years before, and it was one of those brilliant days when the summer wind came blowing in from across the sea, and we were on the road, and the top was down, and we waved our arms as conductors while Sinatra sang "The Coffee Song."

Way down among Brazilians,
Coffee beans grow by the millions.

And I never felt more alive.

And that was Sinatra, the best who had ever sung, the best who had ever swung, because he meant all of it. He meant every word, every syllable, every breath, every crack of the voice, every knockdown, cuckoo, groovy bit of it. He wore vagabond shoes. He was a kind of poet. He was up and down and over and out. He wished he was in love again. That's what made Sinatra. That's what we lost when the Chairman died after a heart attack.

Nobody else cared so much.

He put everything into every song. No matter how melancholy you would ever feel, your darkest time, Sinatra was sadder. He released the album "Frank Sinatra Sings for Only the Lonely" while he pined for Ava Gardner. It was a collection of sad songs for losers — "Willow Weep for Me," "Blues in the Night," "Guess I'll Hang My Tears out to Dry." Sinatra himself would say they should have included a .22-caliber gun with the record.

But then, no matter how delirious you felt, your best day, your glorious moment, Sinatra was happier, swinging to the best song ever recorded, "The Way You Look Tonight," breezing through "Fly Me to the Moon," laughing and scatting "The Lady Is a Tramp," kicking through "I Get a Kick out of You," gazing into "Moonlight in Vermont."

He didn't write the songs. He just ached through them, celebrated through them, and sometimes it was pure genius. Nobody ever hit the hugeness of New York, the thrill of a lucky streak, the agony of a breakup, the sweetness of being in love like Sinatra.

He lived the life, killing night after night with Deano and Sammy, drinking Jack Daniel's, loving too much, and it all just poured out of him. Put it this way: Nobody else could have sung "My Way" and made it work.

And sometimes, he was pure schlock, like when he cooed through the drivel of "Send in the Clowns." He sang those words with all the heart and soul he put into every song, and so he worked so hard rhyming "doors" and "yours," so that neither word sounded right, Sinatra suddenly sounded like a New York cabbie, and you couldn't help but laugh through the saddest part.

Always, though, he was there, all of him, nothing hidden, nothing held back. You were getting the full Sinatra in every song, everything he had, and he had more than anyone else.

He used to say the kids today won't get off their butts and just sing a song, and he was right. There were others who grabbed America for a while, Elvis Presley and the Beatles and Elton John and Madonna, but none of them who could get off their butts and sing a song like Sinatra did.

I saw him in concert a couple of years ago, just before his 80th birthday party. He wasn't Sinatra anymore. He read the lyrics off giant TelePrompTers. He skipped an entire verse of "My Kind of Town." His voice, which had lived its own life as a pirate, a poet, a pauper trailed off, as if it did not have the strength to go on.

And then Sinatra sang "New York, New York." His song. And in that moment, when those little-town blues were melting away, Sinatra was young again. The voice was brilliant again. And in that instant, with a big band banging and crashing, and Sinatra in a tuxedo singing about New York, there was no place on earth as perfect. He made us feel like that.

And when he had hit the last note, he looked at the crowd, waved and said, "You're the best audience I've ever worked for," the same words he had said to audiences for 50 years. Then he left us.

He had given us everything he had to give.

— May 16, 1998

VII

L O V E   T R A N S C E N D E N T

There are lessons in these games, stuff to live by. Never throw a chest-high change-up to Cal Ripken. Never give Joe Montana the ball with too much time. Never taunt Michael Jordan. Judge a ballpark by its mustard. Never leave a beer too close to your feet. Don't ignore the guy who wants a dollar to watch your car outside of Yankee Stadium.

Pro boxers are usually nice. Pro tennis players are usually jerks. Pro wrestling masked men never get the girl.

Yes, there are lessons everywhere in sports, but that has nothing to do with love. There are few love lessons in sports. That's a problem because today I marry Margo Ann, my love, and though I've been living for 31 years, though I've muddled through Shakespeare's sonnets and tried to find meaning in Springsteen and "Casablanca," and Gatsby and the early episodes of "The Love Boat," (before Julie flipped out), truth is, I'm a sportswriter. I talk like one, eat like one, think like one, dress like one no matter what. Today, in a pressed, black Armani tuxedo, I will look like Don Zimmer.

So, I keep trying to find the lesson somewhere in sports, something to guide us through the years. Sports doesn't necessarily bring men and women closer, let's be honest here. I remember one guy, John, who was a baseball nut case, one of those cut-the-box-scores-out-of-*The Sporting News* people, the kind of guy who really was scoring at home, and we imagined how he would meet his true love, and it went like this:

John would be sitting in the bleachers, scoring the game. And, across the aisle, past the beer vendor, he would see her. She would see him. Their eyes would meet, and each would turn away, embarrassed. Only then she would walk up to him, pencil behind her ear, shy smile.

"Excuse me," she would say. "Did you mark that as a hit or an error?"

John never found that woman, of course. There aren't many great love stories in sports. Friends get married, and suddenly they don't have time to watch sports anymore. They don't get out to the ballpark much anymore.

That shouldn't happen with Margo. She loves sports. We met on the basketball court, our first date was a baseball game, she is proud owner of a gigantic Kansas State wood carving her uncle made for her. Still, let's face it, sports and love don't mix well.

The big sports love story out there is the one between former Cincinnati Reds manager Ray Knight and pro golfer Nancy Lopez. Every so often, Ray would caddy for Nancy in tournaments, and, without fail, she would play horribly. Ray is a wonderful guy, but he's a bit hyper, and it seems he would drive her insane with little bits of advice, thoughts, ideas, brainstorms, mixing and tossing her mind, popping fuses, making it just about impossible for her to swing a golf club without falling down.

"Buddy," Ray used to tell me, "sometimes, in a marriage, you need to learn when to shut up."

W.H. Auden it ain't, but it seems pretty good advice. Then there are the words of Royals manager Tony Muser who said, "Find yourself a woman who is five times smarter than you, then spend your life trying to catch up." I've done that, at least. Margo, I love you dearly, and will for as long as there are games to play, athletes to admire, children who run.

Dan Quisenberry was asked for the lesson. He has brain cancer. It wrecks him. He has always been so good at putting thoughts into words, he has always known how to sum up.

"What's the lesson here, Dan?"

Lesson? Can there be lesson in something so terrible? Quisenberry paused for a long, long time. He wanted to say something meaningful, something poetic, but lesson? Finally, he smiled. Something had come to him. He clenched the hand of Janie Quisenberry.

"Love your wife," he said.

— June 5, 1998

OLYMPIC STRUGGLE

SYDNEY — Everyone is fascinated by him. It's so weird. Here we are at the Olympics, where gymnasts fold themselves into origami, where weightlifters lift Buicks over their heads, where long jumpers fly, where even pingpong balls move so fast they could kill a man — or at least make him shout "Ow!" really loud.

Still, everyone is fascinated by him.

"Did you see him?" people ask on the Sydney streets.

He is Eric Moussambani. He almost drowned in an Olympic pool. OK, just kidding. He just took forever to swim 100 meters.

"I want to continue swimming," Moussambani said. "I like the

Olympics."

I can't tell you why this story fascinates everyone. But it does. There are archers nailing bull's-eyes and badminton players hitting birdies 238 million mph and judo fighters who can break your arm just by staring at you.

But the most amazing footage of these Games has been Moussambani flopping, splashing, clawing those last 10 meters as he tried to finish the 100 freestyle Tuesday. A crowd of 17,500 screamed and cheered as if he were Ian Thorpe.

"Did you see him?" people ask everywhere you go.

Moussambani finished in a time of 1:52.72. How slow is that? Well, it's three times slower than the world record. How slow? According to USA Swimming, 80 percent of the 10-and-under girls in the U.S. swim faster than that. How slow? I really, honestly believe I could beat him in a race.

Normally, I'm not too crazy about watching Olympic athletes who are worse at their sport than I am. But there's something about Moussambani. He grew up in Equatorial Guinea, which has not been what you would call a swimming supercenter. There's not a single Olympic-sized pool in the entire country. Moussambani learned to swim earlier this year in crocodile-infested waters.

He did his training at a small hotel pool along with guests who had those inflatable life preservers wrapped around their arms.

His mother, Lucia Malonga, says Eric quit everything he ever tried. He tried soccer. Quit. Basketball. Quit. Running. Quit. But there was something about swimming. Moussambani kept on going to training every single day. He had the Olympics on his mind.

Now, what he did at training is beyond me. He admits he never before swam 100 meters in his life. Apparently these training sessions included chicken fights, a little splashing, a couple of hours of iced-tea drinking on a raft. You probably didn't hear any Rocky music playing at these grueling Moussambani training sessions.

Moussambani showed up in Sydney fully intending to swim the 50 freestyle. That was his event. He could do it without sinking. But his coach — and, really, it's kind of hard to believe he has a coach — made a last-minute change and asked Moussambani to swim the 100 instead.

"I didn't know," Moussambani says, "if I could make it."

He meant that literally. He swam the first 50 meters in 40.97 seconds, which is really, really slow by world-class standards, but not slow enough to make him a worldwide icon. No, it was the second 50 meters that secured Moussambani's place in Olympic history. He paddled and kicked and attacked the water — and he did not seem to be moving.

There's no telling why, even now, watching Eric Moussambani try to finish that second 50 meters is so compelling. But it is. It's incredible to watch. There are people here who say his struggle captures the spirit of the Olympic Games and blah blah blah, but I'm not buying that. There's no way the spirit of the Olympics is found in a guy who can barely swim.

There are people who watch because it's like one of those sports bloopers tapes, you know, the kind where the baseball takes the funny hop and hits the guy in the groin. Ha ha!

But I think it's something else. You have all these amazing athletes here, and they are incredible to watch. But we can't really identify with them. We can't really know what it's like to blur through 100 meters or get dunked on by Vince Carter or fall off the balance beam after four years of torturous training or stand in a boxing ring with someone who can throw 47 punches in a blink of an eye.

But we can understand this, trying to finish a 100-meter swim, just trying to touch the wall even though we're exhausted, in great pain. The crowd is cheering. The wall seems to be running away. This we can understand.

"I want to come back to the Olympics," Moussambani says.

Who can blame him? Moussambani says he will get a new coach and go back into training. He will be splashing in that hotel pool every day. Who knows what he might do in four years?

— Sept. 21, 2000

FRANK WHITE

Frank White comes from a time when baseball could save your life, maybe even your soul, and so he doesn't much like what the kids are doing to his game. They don't dive violently forward to break up the double play. They take days off. They don't lift each other's spirits or demand enough from each other. A player says he's hurt, for instance, and he doesn't want to play. In Frank White's days, those words led to a dozen teammates wandering across the locker room, asking what's wrong, poor little baby, what you got there, a little boo boo? Pushing and prodding and insulting and cursing and persisting until the player, red-faced, livid, stomped into the manager's office and insisted his way back into the lineup.

That's the way they did things when Frank White was young.

"This is such a great baseball town," White says. "I've lived here since I was a kid. I've seen it. People in Kansas City are very forgiving. They don't ask a lot. They want to win, sure, everybody wants to win. But they just want players who play the game hard. They want players who work hard, who run out ground balls, who break up double plays, who make great plays, who play the game right. They want players they can believe in."

White pauses here. He smiles. He is a coach now, the Kansas City Royals first-base coach, the guy who slaps players on the back after singles, the one who warns them when a pitcher suddenly throws to first base. He wears his old No. 20, a number no one else will ever wear because it has been retired. White is 47 years old now, a Kansas City legend.

He smiles because surely, if he was nothing else, Frank White was a player people believed in.

You choose.

There's the romantic version of Frank White's life or the real version, it's your choice. The stories are not that different.

ROMANTIC: Frank White grew up in the shadow of old Municipal Stadium, where the Kansas City Athletics used to play and lose on muggy afternoons when baseball was the only game in town.

REALITY: Nah. Frank White lived 10 blocks away, but he did go to school at Lincoln High, which was right across the street from the old stadium, and sometimes he and his friends would climb to the top of the high school bleachers, munch Arthur Bryant's french fries, sip Vess Cola, and see what they could see over the stadium walls.

"It was a good way to grow up," White says.

ROMANTIC: White grew up in the depths of urban Kansas City, a hard childhood, infused with gangs and drugs, but he was saved by baseball.

REALITY: OK, White doesn't remember any of that. He remembers home, family, friends, street corners, Motown sounds, maybe a few fistfights which swirl in hazy childhood memories. More than that, he remembers the baseball games. They would take old dolls, tear off the heads, wrap them in tape. Old doll heads made pretty good baseballs.

Then Frank White and his pals would play baseball games deep into the night. Sometimes they played at Spring Valley Park, other times at Crews Park, sometimes with friends, sometimes with kids from the other neighborhood. They played hardball, with mosquitoes dancing in their faces, grass stains on the ball, cracked bats. They played so close to Municipal Stadium that maybe, well, sure, they felt close to the Major Leagues. They felt like someday they would play in that stadium. It was too easy to imagine. Kids dreamed like that in those days.

ROMANTIC: White, who never played high school baseball, was working in a steel mill when Royals owner Ewing Kauffman plucked him out and put him in the Royals Baseball Academy. White developed into the best second baseman of his era, maybe the best defensive second baseman who ever lived.

REALITY: Whoa, slow down. True, Frank White did not play high school baseball — baseball wasn't a school sport at Lincoln — but he played for years in the Ban Johnson and Casey Stengel leagues. Urban areas were not scouted too thoroughly in those days, so nobody noticed White. He did not mind. He could play recreation ball until he was 21, and he had a pretty good job at the Metal Protection Plating Company on Truman Road.

But childhood dreams don't just drift away. The Royals held a tryout camp, and White went, just for kicks. He never expected the call asking him to go to the inaugural year of the Royals' Baseball Academy. When the call came, he was already married. He had no interest in going to some snake-infested field in Florida where ground balls skipped off rocks and drill sergeants explained the theories of the double-play pivot. Still, when you've hit doll-head home runs to the faint echo of a Municipal Stadium crowd, well, maybe something gets inside.

"I told my wife that I didn't want to go," White says. "She said, 'You will spent the rest of your life kicking yourself if you don't give it a try.' I knew she was right. But I'm serious, I did not want to go."

There's no romanticizing the old Royals Baseball Academy. It produced a whole bunch of major leaguers, Ron Washington among them, but it was the army, plain and simple. There was curfew, and 6 a.m. bugle calls, and classes and machines that would spit out ground ball after ground ball, tirelessly, endlessly, until the fielder could feel his body sagging.

Ewing Kauffman's idea was that baseball players can be made. Take a talent, raw, crude, unpolished, and you nurture him, mold him, pound him. Frank White hated every single minute of his 18 months at the Baseball Academy. But Ewing Kauffman was right. Frank White came to Sarasota as a first baseman without power. When Frank White left Sarasota, he was the quickest, smartest, most acrobatic second baseman anyone had ever seen.

"I don't think anybody embodied Mr. Kauffman's idea of the academy more than Frank White," says Royals general manager Herk Robinson. "He was such a gifted athlete. He had a great heart. He wanted to play baseball. And he was able to make it his life."

White looks back at the stories, the reality and romance of his life, and he laughs.

"I'm not going to lie to you, it was torture," he says. "I was away from my family. I hated all the rules. There was nothing to do. In my spare time I used to go out to that machine and field more ground balls. That's all there was to do out there. But I guess it made me into something."

The first day that Frank White trotted out to be the Royals first-base coach back in July, he did not know where to stand. He did not know how to react. People began cheering him, they chanted his name, and he stood there red-faced, alone, offering weak little waves to everybody.

"I was over there waving like Gomer Pyle," White says. "You know, 'Howdy. Howdy. Howdy.' That kind of thing. I had to go on the road and become a little more professional. I learned how to give the one big wave and move on."

Truth is, Frank White enjoys being beloved in his hometown. It wasn't that way when he began. He replaced Cookie Rojas, who was wildly popular in Kansas City, and people booed the hometown kid. That hurt. Over the years the marriage between White and his hometown has been beautiful and painful, he has felt betrayed and beloved. Nobody played the game harder. Certainly nobody has ever played defense any better. Frank White won eight Gold Gloves at second base — Gold Gloves are given each year to the best defensive player at each position — and there were times with glove and throw that Frank White resembled an artist.

"He was a beautiful baseball player," teammate George Brett says. "I mean, you look at other guys, and they were great ballplayers. But Frank was something else, you know? He could do things you wouldn't believe. And he was smooth. He was so smooth."

"Yeah, I was the kind of player who you appreciated over time," White says. "I wasn't the best hitter, and I wasn't the fastest runner. But I was fast enough, I hit well enough. And after awhile people realized they could count on me. I was always out there, always playing hard, always doing the things to help the team win."

The appreciation has been there and then gone. There have been times Frank White felt loved, other times forgotten. He left Kansas City to coach with the Boston Red Sox for a while, and he was not sure he wanted to return. Herk Robinson called to talk, asked him to come back, and White felt torn. He loved his hometown. He loved his Royals. But somehow he was not sure he could come home again. Even after returning to Kansas City to work in the Royals community relations department, he refused to pitch batting practice or go down to the field.

"When I called him to be a coach, I wasn't sure what he was going to say," Robinson says.

"I thought about it pretty hard," White says. "I thought I was burned out on coaching. But, there's one thing you find out in baseball. When they ask you, it's a pretty special thing. It's not like that. They don't come to you very often. So, they asked, and I did it. I don't know. It's something to wear the old uniform again."

He wears old No. 20 again, but it's different. The team loses. The fans don't show up in the same numbers. This season the Royals played some of their worst baseball ever, certainly worse than anything White experienced as a player. "We've got some good young players," White says. "But it has been one bad thing after another. We can't get any momentum. We can't get anything going."

White says the team needs a leader. He says the team needs several leaders. He wishes there were more players like the ones he idolized as a young player, the ones who played hard and talked hard and coaxed teammates and just plain won baseball games.

"People don't play baseball like they did in my day, no," White says. He tries to teach the kids to play ball. Some listen. Some don't. At least each day, win or lose, White can hear the Kansas City cheers.

Frank White doesn't know any great tricks to save baseball. That's the stuff owners come up with, player representatives, agents, marketers, people who never played the game. They want to realign the divisions, tear apart the American and National Leagues, add some playoff games, make it all a bit more fun and exciting for the kids. Make it more like a video game or MTV.

Maybe they're right. Maybe the game moves too slowly to grab the kids anymore. "I don't know," White says. "I still think it's the best game in the world. You know, times have changed, but the game hasn't. There are still four balls in a walk, three strikes you're out, 90 feet between the bases. Perceptions have changed, maybe. The player-fan relationship has changed. But baseball is still baseball. It's still the best game."

He thinks Kansas City will fall for the Royals again, maybe when the team begins to play Royals baseball again. He remembers what it was like in 1985, when the Royals played St. Louis in the World Series, when this whole darned city was alive and wild and free.

"Nobody talked about money then," he says. "It wasn't about money or fame or anything like that. You can't understand what it was like to come out to the ballpark, and the whole city was behind you, and you felt all this pressure and all this adrenaline. It was amazing. It can be like that again."

It's not like that now. He sees a rift between the team and urban Kansas City, the same kind of rift that flows all through baseball.

"We have to have more black managers and people in power to let everybody know it's their game too," he says.

He sees a bigger rift between the players and the fans. "People don't even see them as players anymore, they see them as salaries," he says. "I don't think the players spend as much time with the fans, signing autographs, being polite, talking to them. It's an entertainment business."

He sees a Royals team which will win soon. "We're not this bad," he says. "We have some really good young players. Johnny Damon. Mike Sweeney. Jermaine Dye. Rod Myers. Yamil Benitez. These will be good players. This will be a team Kansas City can rally behind."

He sees baseball getting big again in Kansas City. "Kansas City is prime for just about anything," he says. "The people in Kansas City are forgiving. They are second-chance type of people .... It has been awhile since baseball has been the No. 1 thing in town, but it will happen again. I believe that."

He doesn't see his own future, though. Herk Robinson, among others, predict that White can be a Major League manager someday. White says if he's asked, he will consider it. You know how it is baseball. When they ask you, well, you've got to consider.

"I'm not sure I'm up for the Pepto-Bismol and sleepless nights," he says. "But you never know."

Frank White's greatest defensive play came in the 1977 playoffs against the New York Yankees. Well, he's not sure if it's his GREATEST play — "I made so many amazing plays," he says — but considering the pressure, the moment, everything else, well, it was the play.

Reggie Jackson was on first base. Lou Piniella or somebody — White forgets the batter — hit a ground ball up the middle.

Somehow White moved toward the ball. Somehow he dove and smothered it. Somehow he flipped it to second base to get Jackson, who looked back at White in absolute awe.

Frank White remembers that look. That's the one which sticks out after 25 years of playing and coaching and learning baseball. Time drifts away, and he gets older, and the kids get younger, and the baseball isn't what it used to be. White shakes his head.

"Some of the kids get it," he says, and he tells more about his young players, the ones who listen to his stories about Arthur Bryant's fries and the snakes at the Baseball Academy and the boos and the cheers and the World Series and the way Reggie Jackson looked at him. He likes the ones who listen, the ones who run hard, the kids who get it. White smiles about that. It has been a few years since Frank White dove to his left or broke up the double play. Somebody else has to keep this wonderful game going in his hometown.

— **Sept. 21, 1997**

THERE'S ONLY LYNETTE

Lynette Woodard wishes she could have had that three-point line, you know, just for a little while. Sure, she scored 3,649 points in her beautiful career, which is the all-time collegiate women's record, but who knows how many she might have scored with that three-point line?

"I didn't shoot much from out there," she says. "But I could have."

These days are just a little bittersweet for Woodard, the former Kansas player and now assistant coach. Part of her — most of her — is so proud of Jackie Stiles, her fellow Kansan, who is on track to become the all-time leading scorer in NCAA women's basketball history.

Stiles embodies everything that Woodard loves about women athletes today. She's proud. She's confident. She's relentless. She's triumphant. That has been such a long journey for young women. To be triumphant on a basketball court. Woodard is so proud.

Still, another part of Woodard feels forgotten.

The NCAA does not recognize Woodard's all-time scoring record, although she had 527 more points than the NCAA record holder, Mississippi Valley State's Patricia Hoskins. Woodard, you see, finished her career the season before the NCAA took over the sport.

As far as women's basketball goes, those are considered the dark ages.

"I get the impression," Woodard says, "that people think there was no women's basketball before it went under the umbrella of the NCAA."

There is something haunting about sports records that are forgotten. You might say they are just numbers on paper, but they are more. They are history. Ask the guy next to you who hit the most home runs in a season, and he will probably tell you Mark McGwire broke the record of Roger Maris, who broke the record of Babe Ruth.

Josh Gibson hit more. People just don't remember.

Yes, Negro Leagues players are forgotten. Hilton Smith. Willard Brown. Ted Strong. Do you know them? Probably not. A big part of that, I think, is because their numbers, their statistics, are lost in time. What if I told you Hilton Smith had a five-year span when he won more than 100 games and lost fewer than 10? Would you believe it?

Every baseball fan can tell you Hank Aaron hit 755 home runs and Joe DiMaggio hit in 56 straight games and Ted Williams hit .406. Biz Mackey? Oscar Charleston? Judy Johnson? Do you know them?

Now, Lynette Woodard's records are being overlooked. What a player she was. She scored more points in her four years than any Division I player of either gender except Pistol Pete Maravich, who had 3,667. She still holds Kansas records in scoring, rebounding, steals — and that's men or women. She was a passer and a shot-blocker, a slasher and a shooter.

Do people know her? Perhaps. Vaguely. She was the first woman to play for the Globetrotters. She was captain of the 1984 Olympic team. But her brilliant college career grows fainter and fainter. All because she played before the NCAA took over.

"There were so many terrific players," Woodard says of those times, and she sounds much like Buck O'Neil, who went town to town for years saying of those Negro Leagues stars, "Man, we could play."

The Women's Basketball Hall of Fame in Knoxville, Tenn., has inducted 49 people already, but not Lynette Woodard. They say it's because she played two seasons in the WNBA, 1997-98, and she has to wait five years after her "playing career" ended to be eligible. But they waived that rule for the ultra-hyped Nancy Lieberman-Cline.

Woodard may have been the best ever — the Willie Mays, the Michael Jordan, the Joe Montana of her sport. And some forget.

Yet, Woodard really doesn't let any of this trouble her. She played basketball for the joy, the thrill of it. And if she was an inspiration to women as diverse as WNBA sensation-turned-coach Cynthia Cooper and my wife Margo, well, that makes her feel good inside.

"Women basketball players are so much more confident now," Woodard says. "That's what's beautiful to see. They are encouraged to play sports from the time when they're little girls. So you see athletes who are just better and prouder and more confident in what they do. That's what I love.

"It was different when I was playing. We were discouraged. We were told that it wasn't our place to play sports. But we played anyway. We played because we loved it."

Woodard says she has never seen Jackie Stiles play in person. But she has seen Stiles on video, and even on tape it all comes through: Stiles' passion, her zeal, her drive, her love of the game.

It's not lost on Woodard that they both grew up playing basketball in Kansas, even if it was in different times.

"Hey, someone scores 3,000 points in a career, and you know she's special," Woodard says. "Jackie is obviously very special. She's so confident in her shot. She thinks she will make every one of them."

That's how Lynette Woodard felt on the court, too. It's still how she feels.

"Yeah, I would have liked having that three-point shot," she says. "I'll bet I would have make a few of those. I'll bet I would have scored a few more points."

— Feb. 11, 2001

WRESTLING SUPERSTAR!

All his life, Denny Kolvek knew he was The Superstar. He knew it deep down, where the most wholehearted of men's dreams rest. So it did not matter that he was customer-service manager for Imagyn Urology, a medical company, as sensible a job as a man can get. It did not matter that he had married Debbie, a sensible accountant. It did not matter that he had turned 31, a sensible age, a time for mortgages and lawnmowers and Lamaze classes.

"I am the SHMACK-DADDY!" Denny Kolvek screamed Saturday in the Golden Eagle Casino in Horton, Kan., and he flexed and he pointed to his wrestling opponent, named "The Icebreaker," or maybe it's just "Icebreaker." The Superstar raised his arms and stomped his feet and stuck out his tongue. The children cheered.

"DO YOU WANT TO SEE ME BEAT THE SHMACK OUT OF THIS GUY?" he screamed to them.

"YEAH!" they screamed back.

"Who's The Superstar?"

"YOU ARE THE SUPERSTAR!"

"Who's The Superstar?"

"YOU ARE THE SUPERSTAR!"

*   *   *

Pro wrestling is a world of babies and heels. Babies are the good guys. Heels are the bad guys. Simple as that. Yes, on television, wrestling gets a little more tangled, good guys are bad guys, bad is good, there is smoke and sparks and innuendo, it's all a bit too clouded, a little too much like real life. But along the folding-chair circuit of small-time wrestling, it's pretty plain. Babies smile. Heels cheat. The referees see nothing. And masked men never get the girl.

"I'm a baby," Denny Kolvek says. He had decided that long ago, about the same time he decided that he would be named The Superstar and that he would have a big blue star cover his face and that he would have fringe on his boots, like the band members of KISS. He knew he would wear heels to add a couple of inches to his 5-foot-8 frame. He knew he would wear blue. Yes, he always knew the pro wrestler within.

Of course, in real life, he was neither a baby nor a heel. He was just a regular guy, like anybody else. He wrestled in high school, back in Omaha, Neb., and even went to a small college in Minnesota to wrestle. He got homesick. He thought he was in love. He went back to Omaha, went to college, tried teaching and coaching for a while but realized there wasn't much money in it. So it goes. He went into insurance. The craziest thing he did was in 1992, when he went to the Olympic freestyle wrestling trials in Del City, Okla., and he finished sixth in his class, a nice moment, but just that, a nice moment.

He moved to Kansas City, worked, umpired softball games on weekends, met Debbie, fell in love for real, got married, and all the while, he let The Superstar grumble softly in his stomach. Then Debbie, the practical one, the sane one, said, "Well, if you really want to wrestle ... "

By the end of the ellipsis, Denny Kolvek was at wrestling school in Texas.

*   *   *

The first thing they teach you in wrestling school, at least the first thing they teach you at the School Of The Squared Circle, in Arlington, Texas, is this: It's your job to make the other guy look good.

Later, they teach you how to hit somebody with a chair.

But first, you have to learn how to make it all real. It's harder than it looks. Denny Kolvek had been wrestling for 15 years, but in those matches he was trying to actually beat the other guy. In pro wrestling, of course, you are working with the other guy, it's a duet, and if you fall right, the other guy looks like a giant. If he falls wrong, you look like a jerk.

"I've been wrestling all my life, and I will tell you, this is much harder," he says. "You have to be in great shape. If you fall wrong, you can get yourself killed in there. Even if you fall right, you will walk out of the ring with bruises and aches and pains. People say, 'But you're just faking.' The pain is real, brother."

There are more than 50 wrestling schools in the United States (and very few in Russia, which might explain the recent drought of mad Russian wrestlers), and all of them teach the basics of the body slam, the choke hold, the clothesline. That is, they teach you how to take all of those moves. Anybody can slam another guy. The great ones get slammed beautifully.

Denny Kolvek showed up at the School of the Squared Circle, and, man, he wanted to learn it all in one day, he wanted to soak it all in, he wanted to get his back slammed on concrete, he wanted to get thrown through a table, he wanted to get kicked in the head and tossed down from the top rope.

"Before Denny even got here he knew what he wanted to be," says Brian Harkrider, a longtime wrestler himself and one of the trainers at the school. "He really wanted this. It must have been a lifelong dream or something."

Kolvek worked during the week. He flew to Arlington on weekends. They taught him the right way to smack a guy's head into the turnbuckle. They showed him the best way to be thrown out of the ring. They taught him all the moves, all the brawling techniques, how to take all the bumps. Back at home, Denny practiced his moves on the waterbed, until, of course, it burst.

"Waterbed," Denny says, shaking his head. "I should have figured that one out."

*   *   *

Sure, there have been mistakes. There was the waterbed thing, of course. Then, Kolvek's first match, a charity thing in St. Joseph, he painted his face with watercolor, which meant that as soon as he started sweating, the paint began running into his eyes. He was The Blind Superstar.

Oh yeah, there was the simple math problem for his first professional match, the one in Port Arthur, Texas.

Travel costs: $300.

Pay: $35.

So, class, what will it cost the Superstar to get stomped by a 260-pound heel with the particularly uninspired name of "Dude"?

"How do you think I feel about all this?" Debbie says. "I'm an accountant. But this is how you have to do it when you're starting out."

This is the world of small-time wrestling. There's glamour and money at the top, for the big boys of wrestling, for the Hulk Hogans and Ric Flairs. But just as the true character of baseball is in the little parks across America, the real heart of the pro wrestling world lies in promotions like "Midwest Empire Wrestling." Midwest Empire or MEW is run by Steve Estes, who spent a colorful 23 years wrestling as the Super Destroyer and then the Assassin, but of course, there was another Assassin, so he became Assassin No. 2, and so on.

Estes has two sons wrestling in his promotions, one who is trying a new effeminate act as "Bashful Brad." He also has a wrestler who walks around with a live snake and a guy named "Bubba," who wears a Kansas State jersey with "Bubba" on the back. One of the star attractions is a tag team called "The Darkside," where one of the wrestlers walks around with a metal chair with the names of all the wrestlers he's conked painted on the back.

The MEW wrestlers go at it in gymnasiums, casinos, clubs, wherever they can get a couple of hundred people to shriek and hiss. It's not the big time, perhaps, but it's still tough to break in. These promotions are usually made up of family, a few friends, a few acquaintances. It's like trying to join the circus.

Denny Kolvek decided to take the business approach. He sent out his photograph, his resume (which let the various promoters know, among other things, that he knew how to brawl outside the ring with chairs, tables, etc.), and perhaps most impressive, a videotape with some wrestling action and a few practice interviews.

"I am the Shmack-Daddy!" he yelled at promoters.

Steve Estes decided to give the guy a chance.

"I liked the way he presented himself," Estes said. "He called me 'Sir.' I liked that. People have called me all sorts of names through the years. I like the young men who are polite and call me 'Sir,' or 'Assassin.' "

*   *   *

The Superstar knew he would have trouble with Icebreaker in Saturday's match, though he really had not met Icebreaker until about an hour before the match. The Superstar was originally supposed to wrestle some green guy named Scott from Wichita, but as they plotted out the match, Scott fell wrong on his shoulder and had to go to the hospital.

"And people say this isn't real," Steve Estes said.

Anyway, that meant The Superstar would face Icebreaker, no pushover, though The Superstar took command early with his uncanny ability to jump off the top rope and land on people. It's quite a disabling move in wrestling, to land on somebody, and while the slot machines rang in the casino, The Superstar just kept landing on Icebreaker, controlling the match.

Then, The Superstar really was controlling the match. Estes had done something relatively unheard of for a new wrestler: He had let Denny Kolvek script his own match. "Make yourself look good," Estes had offered. So Kolvek decided to let The Superstar dominate the match with his aerial moves until, well, until Icebreaker kicked him in the general groin area.

That's wrestling. Heels will kick in the general groin area.

That infuriated the crowd, especially the 50 or so kids who simply could not believe the referee would miss so blatant a foul. What, was this the Kansas State-Nebraska football game? "Give us a new referee," a little boy yelled, and around him everyone booed and shrieked as Icebreaker had his way for a while, tossing The Superstar all over the ring, smacking his face, sapping all of his energy.

The Superstar seemed finished, but then, suddenly, amazingly, he was up, full of pep, bouncing around the ring, asking the crowd for help, and then he slammed Icebreaker, jumped on him, pinned him, his first victory ever, and the crowd loved it, and Denny Kolvek's mother cheered, his mother-in-law cheered too, some of his friends from work, and, loudest of all, his wife, Debbie.

"He's a trip, isn't he?" she asked sometime later, and by then, Denny Kolvek was signing autographs for the kids, sticking his tongue out at them, calling them each his little Shmack-Daddies. One of the children asked him whether he had ever been hurt by the lawless tactics of the Icebreaker.

"Yeah," The Superstar said. "I was very hurt. But you can't ever give up. You've got to keep fighting."

The kid seemed content with that answer. The Superstar kept on signing autographs. Denny Kolvek would have to go back to work Monday, real work, but he would not think about all that, no sir, not while in his wonderful world of babies and heels and assassins and chairs that might hit you in the head.

"You've got to follow that dream," he said. "Even if that dream is insane."

— **April 26, 1999**

D E A R   M R .   P R E S I D E N T

You don't even know how this pardon request reached your desk. You're the president of the United States of America, by gosh, and you might have time to consider, say, a billionaire who gave loads of money to a friendly nation or the son of the education secretary or maybe your brother. People like that.

But this? A man who sold crack to an undercover officer four separate times? Please. And there was a gun. And it all happened near a school. And the guy's only defense was that he sold her the junk because he wanted to get her into bed. Now, how does something like this get to the desk of the president? Someone on your staff must have fallen asleep. You reach instantly for the "Pardon Denied" stamp — if there is such a thing — because you don't have time for this. You have 20 million more presidential things to do. You raise the stamp high above your head, bring it down hard, only then, just an instant before stamp smacks paper, maybe, you catch the name on the request.

The name is Willie Mays Aikens.

Willie Mays Aikens?

The ballplayer?

*   *   *

The doctor came up with the name. That was Oct. 14, 1954, less than two weeks after the World Series ended. Less than two weeks after the first charmed season of Willie Mays. Say hey. What a player. Mays hit home runs, stole bases, chased fly balls all over New York. The doctor suggested the name, Willie Mays. He figured that this baby without a father, born in a little South Carolina town called Seneca, might be blessed by it.

Twenty-six years later to the day, Willie Mays Aikens played in his first World Series game. He hit two home runs. In the fourth game of that 1980 World Series, he hit two more home runs. Nobody had ever done that before in a World Series, not even Willie Mays. Nobody has done it since.

Guilty? Affirmative, Mr. President. He's guilty as sin. No need to call the FBI. Willie Aikens sold 63 grams of crack to an undercover officer. He was a pathetic figure. He wasn't even 40, but he looked about 78. Weighed more than 300 pounds. Addicted to the core. You couldn't tell where the drugs stopped and Willie began.

He did crazy things. Once, his girlfriend claimed he dragged her down the stairs. Aikens pleaded guilty to that. Once, he was charged with trying to bribe a guy $100 to get him out of a drug test. He pleaded guilty to that, too.

Does it matter that before, when he was young, his teammates unanimously loved him? Such a sweet guy when he wasn't high.

"He had a lot of laughing in him," former Royals star Frank White said. "He was just one of those guys who, when he started laughing, everybody around him started laughing. You just wanted to be around him."

The cocaine ripped Aikens apart. He got hooked in California, free-basing while playing with the Angels. Then, in Kansas City, cocaine became part of his daily routine. He got high in the late morning, then before games ran furious laps to sweat out the junk. He got high again at night. He was arrested for drugs in 1983, along with three Royals teammates, and he served three months in Texas. After that, major-league teams really didn't want much to do with him. He went to play ball in Mexico, and one year in Puebla, he hit .454 with 46 home runs and 154 RBIs. They still talk about that year in Puebla. Then, Willie Mays Aikens could always hit.

Guilty? Affirmative, Mr. President. For a long time, Aikens at least could hit. That helped fill his days. But when baseball ended, all he had was the high. Police caught him with drug paraphernalia in 1992, but the truth is they could have caught him any day and twice on Sunday. Cocaine was his life.

"He was such a good guy you wanted to believe he would beat it," said his former agent and longtime friend Ron Shapiro. "But he never got to the root of the problem. He would not come to grips."

Police said they heard complaints of heavy traffic around Aikens' Kansas City home. An undercover officer went to check it out. She drove up, asked Aikens for directions. Aikens plainly tried to pick her up. She called him a couple of times. He kept trying to pick her up. She mentioned drugs. Aikens told her that he could get her all she wanted.

And that was that. She asked him to get her drugs. He did. She asked him to cook it into crack. He did. The officer kept going back — four times total — until he had sold her enough crack to score major jail time.

Then, the police closed in.

"I'm a drug addict, I'm not a drug dealer," Aikens pleaded in court.

The judge sentenced Aikens to 20 years and 8 months in prison. With good behavior, the sentence could be knocked down to a little more than 17 years.

When Willie Aikens played in Toronto, he would sometimes go talk to recovering alcoholics. It was hard for him, partly because his stepfather was an abusive alcoholic, partly because he never fully mastered the stuttering that had troubled him since he was a kid. And, of course, Willie Aikens liked to drink. And, of course, he had not kicked cocaine.

Still, he spoke from the heart.

"I've made a lot of mistakes," he told them. "Don't make the mistakes I made."

*   *   *

Nobody claims that Willie Aikens actually used a gun in the drug sale. He owned a gun, yes, but it was so unobservable that the undercover officer never once mentioned it in her police reports. Only after the police searched the house and found the gun did she file a special report.

Aikens got slapped with five years for using a gun in a drug sale.

Then, there is no mercy in the law for people involved with crack, Mr. President. There may be mercy for embezzlers and tax evaders and even people who sell other drugs, like powder cocaine (which has the same chemical structure) but not crack. You remember, America went into crack hysteria back in the '80s — crack babies in the news every day — and a law was passed to slam crack addicts and dealers, to punish them at 100 times the rate of cocaine offenders.

Willie Aikens sold 63 grams of crack to an undercover officer, about 2.2 ounces, enough for at least 500 doses. He swears he never sold to anyone else.

He was sentenced as if he had sold 15 pounds of cocaine, enough for at least 50,000 doses.

"If you want to punish the crime, punish the crime," said Marcia Shein, an attorney in Atlanta who tried unsuccessfully to get Aikens' sentence reduced. "But if Willie Aikens had sold powder to the officer, he would be out already. Instead, with good behavior, he's looking at another 11 years."

Crack vs. powder has become one of the hottest issues in American law. Many judges, lawyers and advocate groups have railed against the 100-to-1 ratio, saying it is unfair and quite possibly racist. Consider that, according to the U.S. Sentencing Committee, more than 90 percent of people charged with crack offenses are black or Hispanic.

"It's like we're going back to the 1950s," said Shein, who is one of the nation's leading advocates for getting the law changed. "How can we live in a country where we punish black crimes 100 times more than white ones?"

Truth is, this already has gone before Congress twice. The House asked the Sentencing Commission to look into this in 1995 and again in 1997. Both times, the Commission recommended significantly lessening the penalties for crack offenses. Both times, they pointed at the unfairness of the law.

Both times, the House voted to keep things as they are.

Let's face it, nobody gets to Congress by being soft on crack.

"The politicians know it's wrong," says U.S. District Court Judge Scott Wright. "If they don't know it's wrong, they're idiots. They're just afraid. They're afraid to appear soft. So, this unfair law goes on."

Willie Aikens is no lawyer. He does not get into the national debate. He has no great insights into the subject. He simply serves his 20-year, 8-month sentence. As author Frank Deford said on National Public Radio: "Serial murderers pull less time."

*   *   *

Willie Aikens may have been the slowest player ever to play for the Royals. He stole three bases in his career. His teammates can remember him running from first to third ... it seemed like the man was running in a bucket of jelly. Mountain ranges moved faster than this guy.

But man, could he hit. That was his gift. He didn't have much growing up, and guys would poke fun at him for his small-town ways, but when he was right, Aikens could hit the baseball anywhere you threw it. He hit .400 in that 1980 World Series. Those Philadelphia pitchers couldn't figure out any way to get him out. He even hit a triple, and man was it something to watch him lumber around those bases.

Here's what his teammates remember most about that Series. Game three, 10th inning, game on the line, Philadelphia's Tug McGraw walked George Brett to get to Aikens. And Aikens promptly smacked an opposite-field single, scoring Willie Wilson and giving the Royals their first-ever World Series victory.

That's how Willie Mays Aikens was, when he was right.

*   *   *

The law can't help him, Mr. President. Late last year, Judge Dean Whipple closed the book on Aikens. Shein made one last desperate attempt to knock some years off Aikens' sentence, but the government put together a strong case, and Judge Whipple ruled as he had to rule. The law is crystal clear. Crack dealers, even small-timers, will do harder time than almost any other kind of criminal. That's America.

"Until the laws are changed," Judge Wright said, "there's just nothing any of us can do."

So Willie Aikens does his hard time. He has graduated from at least three different drug programs and says he has been drug-free for six years. Friends say he's back to being the sweet guy he was before drugs turned him inside out. He is back to his playing weight, maybe even a little less. Aikens also says he has found religion. Yes, Mr. President, that's a familiar story — inmate finds God — but his friends say there's a serenity about Willie Aikens.

"This wasn't an evil man," Shapiro said. "This wasn't a pusher. This was a man who had a weakness, who did terrible things because of that weakness. It took incarceration to get him to come to grips with who he is. ... It's not like he had to be remade. He has always been a good man."

Shapiro is the one who sent the pardon request to your desk, Mr. President. In the letter, he writes much of what you just read, and he mentions that Aikens has two daughters who are growing up and a mother who is dying. He includes letters from more than a dozen people, some of them old ballplayers, like Hal McRae and Dusty Baker and Jim Fregosi and Bobby Richardson. They all vouch for Aikens' character. Several prominent journalists — including Deford and HBO's Bryant Gumbel — have appealed for leniency in this case.

Then, there's a letter from Aikens himself. He calls himself Willie M. Aikens. He doesn't use his full name.

"I did commit some crimes while I was using drugs," he wrote. "I have done something about my drug problem .... I made some bad choices in my life which led to my incarceration. Does the time of 20 years fit the crime I committed?"

*   *   *

In Article II, Section II of the U.S. Constitution, it says the president of the United States "shall have Power to Grant Reprieves and Pardons for Offenses against the United States." There are no rules there, no guidelines even, it all comes down to whether or not the president looks your way with mercy in his heart.

On Jan. 20, two hours before leaving office, President Clinton pardoned 140 people and commuted 36 sentences. Among the 176 were numerous drug offenders, a handful of disgraced politicians, Patty Hearst, the president's brother, and, of course, the now-famous Marc Rich.

Aikens was not on the list.

He remains in Atlanta Federal Penitentiary. He is all out of appeals. Aikens sold 2.2 ounces of crack to an officer when he was a lost soul. He is paying for it with his life. Willie Mays Aikens will be at least 56 years old when he's released from prison unless an American president, maybe even the current president, an old baseball owner, has mercy in his heart for an old ballplayer.

— **March 25, 2001**

SO THIS IS FISHING

(An outing on the water with wife, Margo, and outdoor writer Brent Frazee)

F athers-in-law. Cecil, my father-in-law, flinched only one time during the entire courtship, bless his heart. Cecil has lived most of his life in a tiny place called Cuba — a suburb to a bump in the road in north central Kansas — but he loves his daughter very much, so he accepted the Cleveland accent. He withstood the Japanese import car. He smiled at the lousy jokes. He looked away when I asked for steak sauce. He even cherished the consonant-crazy Polish name.

"So, you fish?" he asked once.

"Uh, no, never caught a fish in my life."

And that was too much. Cecil grimaced. He couldn't help it. He got this look on his face — this 'what-the-heck-kind-of-guy-is-my-daughter-marrying?' look — and he asked many questions ("What about bass? Caught any bass? Any crappie? How about a sunfish?"). Soon after, he regained his composure and returned to his genial ways.

On the eve of our wedding, I gave my future wife a pair of pearl earrings. She gave me a Shimano fishing rod and a tackle box.

*   *   *

Brent. Brent has a fishing scanner. This, I've got to believe, is cheating. I mean, first off, we're out on the lake at 6:30 a.m. on a Sunday. Heck, if you wake me up at 6:30 a.m. on a Sunday and dangle a shiny hook in front of my mouth, I'm going to bite at it too.

Second, it's not like a fish is James Bond. Heck, we've been pulling pretty much the same trick on fish since the beginning of time, and they keep falling for it. You would think they would have a meeting or distribute pamphlets saying, "If you see floating worms or shiny metal objects, don't bite." But no. Fish need better leadership.

So I'm thinking that the scanner is overkill, but Brent wanted to be sure. Brent is a serious fisherman. Your basic fishermen go out on the water to drink beer, to talk about sports, to drink beer, to get a tan, to drink beer. Brent goes out to catch fish.

"There are fish here," he said, pointing to the scanner, and indeed there were pretty blue fish on the scanner. There were none biting, but they looked good.

"There are fish here," he said again.

*   *   *

Fishing is easy. It took about four seconds to reel in the first fish of my life. There wasn't much fight there. He was a bass, barely bigger than the lure that Brent had given me. In fact, I thought it was the lure Brent had lent me, until Brent pulled a fish off the line. I named him Bob.

"It's not a good idea," Brent said, "to name the fish."

"This is one dumb fish," Brent said, but, let's be honest here, Brent was really just covering up for his disappointment that I was catching everything. The guy had his whole column written before I got there, the one about the goofy city slicker pulling in weeds and getting terrorized by mosquitoes. Joke's on him. I pulled in fish and got terrorized by mosquitoes.

*   *   *

Cleaning fish. The thing about fishing is it's all "A River Runs Through It" until you have to clean the things. There's a pleasant job, huh? Suddenly, the apartment smells like the galley of the pirate ship Starkist, there's fish mush everywhere, and for what? The fish themselves are bonier than Rog from the old "What's Happening" show.

Brent says you should soak the fish overnight in 7 Up or saltwater to get rid of the "fishy" taste, and there's a ringing endorsement. You'll notice there are no recipes telling you to soak a chocolate cake overnight to get rid of the "chocolaty" taste.

Anyway, bottom line, filleting fish is pretty gross, and it's a good thing I hadn't named any of them beforehand.

*   *   *

The aftermath. So the question is: Am I a changed man? Well, I do have 29 mosquito bites on my right leg, and my freezer smells like Long John Silver. But I'm also getting respect from Brent, who wants to take me around the country in some sort of Paul Newman - Tom Cruise fishing hustle.

And there's a new edge in the voice of Cecil, who now understands just what a prize he has for a son-in-law. Scary thing is now he keeps talking about bagging us an elk, and I have absolutely no idea what he's talking about.

— July 19, 1998

VIII

HUG EVERYBODY YOU CAN

Buck O'Neil turns 88 years old on Saturday. Lord, he looks good. He feels good, too. He's lived all these years, through segregation and heartbreak and wild parties and sweet love and nationwide fame and all those baseball games, thousands and thousands of them, and he's happy now to give out his tips for dealing with the millennium.

He asks one thing in return: Join the Negro League Baseball Museum. Buck O'Neil has spent so much of his wonderful life telling people about the Negro Leagues. He doesn't tell much of the sad stuff. He doesn't talk much about racism or the names they called him or the unfairness of it all. Just a little. Mostly, he talks about the fun and the players and the warm afternoons and the glorious baseball they played before Jackie Robinson came along. He is baseball's greatest spokesman, one of sports' greatest men, and this is his pride, this is his heart, this great little museum in his hometown.

If you don't know, the museum is over there at 18th and Vine, and less than 25 percent of the members are from Kansas City. Shame, shame. This is one of Kansas City's treasures; we should embrace it.

Now, in his own words, Buck O'Neil's tips for the millennium:

First of all, don't worry about the millennium. Don't worry none. Everything will be just fine. You can't spend your life worrying about things. I'm not worried. I'm already thinking about what I'm going to do the next millennium.

You know what Satchel Paige used to say. He said, "Don't look back because something might be gaining on you." Well, I'm 88 years old. That something hasn't caught me yet.

Hug everybody you can, especially the pretty women.

Drain the bitterness out of your heart. My daddy was a good man. He paid his taxes. He lived a good life. But he couldn't vote. He was not bitter, though. No. And now, look, they made Saturday "Buck O'Neil Day." We've come a long way to do that. A long way.

Sing a little every day.

Do yourself a favor: Go down to 18th and Vine just to see a bit of Kansas City history. It was exciting. Yeah. There were musicians and baseball players and beautiful women and men dressed up like you wouldn't believe. Every restaurant, hotel and bar had a band playing sweet music. Yeah. People ask me what it was like, I tell them this: A man would come to Kansas City and say "I have a cousin here, but I don't know where he is." I would say "Well, you just stand right here on the corner of 18th and Vine, and before this day is over, he will show up." Yeah. That was 18th and Vine.

Don't smoke any of those leaves or put anything up your nose.

Tell people you love them.

Listen to old people tell stories. They might teach you something.

Do a little showboating every now and again in your life. Remember, it was the so-so ballplayers that came up with the word "Showboating." They were jealous. If you have something to show, go ahead and showboat a little bit.

Don't be jealous of any other city. Kansas City is the greatest city on earth.

Be there for old friends.

Always be on time. There's no use in being late.

Don't let anger boil up inside you. There's too much anger out there already. Yeah. Too much anger.

Root for the Royals. They're a good young team. They make you feel alive because they play so hard. That's what baseball is all about.

Hold hands with the person next to you. That way they can't get away. And neither can you.

Learn your history. It's a wonderful history. So many wonderful things have happened in the last 100 years. We have come so far. We still have a ways to go, but that's your job, you and your children and their children. We will get there. I know it.

Live a long life. Yeah. You get to see a whole lot that way. A whole lot.

— **Nov. 12, 1999**

ROY WILLIAMS ON A TOUGH LOSS

O KLAHOMA CITY — Question: How hard was last year's tournament loss to Arizona, Roy?

*   *   *

The smile.

Kansas coach Roy Williams smiles. It's not his happy smile. No, you don't see Roy Williams' happy smile at news conferences. You see Roy Williams' happy smile in certain places, certain times, like on the golf course after a good shot, or when he's in the swirl of basketball talk with coaching friends, or, most likely, on the court, with his kids.

Sure, that's when he feels free, when he's alone with his team. He can smile. He can be angry. He can be sad. He can be himself, all his warts, all his insecurities, all his joy, sure, he can yell or cry or dance. Yeah, did you see him dance on top of the ladder after Kansas won the Big 12 championship? So what if he looked goofy. Did you see the kids laugh? Did you see the way their eyes lit up?

No, he can't smile like that at a news conference. These are reporters. They twist his words sometimes, some maliciously, most carelessly. One the other day had asked his kids after the victory over Nebraska in the Big 12 tournament: "Coach Williams says this feels like a loss. How do you feel?" Well, dadgum it, he hadn't said that stuff about it feeling like a loss. He hadn't said anything like that. Where do they come up with this stuff?

No, he gives them that other smile, the weary smile, the camera smile, the public smile, the same smile he has given them the 500 other times he has answered this question and all the others like it. This is not his happy smile. He's never happy to be talking about himself. He's just doing his job.

"Well..." he begins.

*   *   *

The accent.

Roy Williams doesn't often hit the high notes on his "I's." No, it's more of a relaxed tone, a doctor's open-your-mouth-wide sound he makes, and he adds a few "Y's," in there, twanging some words, and it all comes out breezily, friendly like, such as "Ah fee-y-eel we're trah-in' to fahnd ourselves, play we-y-ell a-yund become a good basketball teeym."

The accent comes from the North Carolina mountains, Williams with it. He grew up in Asheville, son of Lallage, who ironed shirts, 10 cents apiece, to keep the family going, son of Mack, who tangled with alcohol, drifted in and out of their lives. The family was poor. Williams found solace in basketball. Roy Williams doesn't like talking about that. There's one story he tells, about being unable to afford a Coca-Cola — pronounced Co-Cola in the Carolinas — when he and his friend stopped at a gas station on the way home from school. Lallage found out, and the next morning, there was a dime on the kitchen table.

Roy Williams keeps cases of Co-Colas in his garage now.

Truth is, the accent gives away about as much as Williams would like to give away. It's a small-town Southern accent, crowded with friendliness, dripping with eagerness, tumbling honesty. The accent tells of the place he's from. People who meet Roy Williams immediately like him. They wonder why. It's the accent.

"There's just a solidness in the way coach Williams talks,"

former point guard Jacque Vaughn says. "He sounds like the most down-to-earth person, and he is the most down-to-earth person."

Some parts of Williams' personality match the accent. He's downright corny at times. You've heard all those gollies, goshes, shucks, dadgums. He begins each practice with a thought for the day, something deep-thoughtish, such as "It's better to chase your dreams than run from your problems." He once put his six seniors on the floor to start Senior Night because, well, he had six seniors.

He hops up and down with his players after championships, though he looks out of place and out of step. He lives in the same house he bought when he came to Lawrence.

Here's a story: Only in the last couple of years has Roy Williams put his name on the door of his office. Before that, the office had read: "Kansas basketball coach." It took Roy Williams eight years as coach before he felt like it was his program, eight years before he felt comfortable putting up his own name. Yes, in so many ways, Williams is that small-town North Carolina kid who breathes basketball and rounds off his "I's."

"Ah don't ree-yeelly lahk talkin' about last year," Williams says.

But the accent covers up something, too.

*   *   *

The hair.

While Williams ponders a way to answer the question, you notice the hair. Roy Williams' is a distinguished gray. Williams had that flop-top hair once, back at North Carolina, when coach Dean Smith had all the headaches. Williams was just a part-time assistant then; he sold North Carolina calendars around the state to make enough money for his family. He sold 22,000 calenders one year, so he and his wife, Wanda, could buy a house.

The gray started creeping into his hair after he took the Kansas job, after he took that 1991 Jayhawks team on their wild NCAA Tournament ride, through Arkansas' pressure defense, through Bob Knight's Indiana, through North Carolina and his hero and role model Dean Smith, all the way to the championship game. That run made Roy Williams famous. The gray started coming in pretty much the next day.

"He is as much of a perfectionist as anyone I know," says Smith, who certainly knows his perfectionists. Williams would sit in the stands when he was a student at North Carolina and watch Smith's Tar Heels practice. He kept notes. Of course, he still has those notes.

From Smith, he learned discipline, fundamentals, the magnitude of details, the right way. He is an amazing stickler. On Senior Night, when the students began chanting, "We want C.B.," for senior C.B. McGrath, he wandered over to them and said, "I'm the coach." They hushed. Friday night, Kansas led Prairie View A&M by 36 at halftime, and Williams began to tick off all the things the Jayhawks had done wrong. "Aren't we being a bit picky?" an assistant coach asked.

"You're dadgum right we're being picky," Williams said.

Yes, Williams is an organizing fanatic, a detail zealot, a controller, but there's something else. Williams also wants to win so badly it tears at his stomach, it clutches at his heart, Wanda has often worried that he would collapse on the sideline. In fact, Roy Williams has blacked out on the sideline. He has the best winning percentage of any active coach, second all-time behind the great Clair Bee. He has averaged an astonishing 29 wins a season in the 1990s.

Still, it is the few losses that have marked him, torn out his insides, turned his hair gray. He takes golf losses hard; you can imagine what basketball losses mean. The question — How hard was last year's tournament on you, Roy? — is very real. It about broke him.

"I'll tell you one difference between coach Williams and me," says Florida State coach and former Williams assistant Steve Robinson. "He has a lot more gray hair."

In the fourth grade — here's another story Williams doesn't mind telling — he had a teacher who put the names of the 10 best students on the board. Forty years later, Roy Williams can still feel the horror of looking at that board and not seeing his name. Losing tortures him.

"I don't want the kids to be like me," he says. "I want them to enjoy themselves. I don't want them not sleeping, not eating, thinking too much. They're kids. They should have fun."

*   *   *

The look.

Roy Williams looks like somebody. He's about ready to really answer the question, he's looking right at the reporter, and he looks like somebody. Who is it? He's got those sad eyes and puffy cheeks, and, well, of course.

He looks like Huckleberry Hound.

He starts to answer the question, but once you see Huckleberry Hound in his face, it's hard to listen. It's hard to imagine Huckleberry Hound taking a loss too hard.

And there's your story. The Huckleberry look, like the smile, like the accent, like the gray hair, it all paints a picture. This is what Roy Williams will let you see. You don't need to know the rest. You don't need to know how last season's loss to Arizona ravaged

Williams. Any loss kills him, but that one was the worst. The Jayhawks won 34 games, were considered the best team in America, but more, he loved that Kansas team — Jacque Vaughn, Scot Pollard, Jerod Haase — those were like his kids. He let them down. He could not bear the agony. He wrote down lists of questions about himself. What could I have done? Did I tighten up? Was I outcoached?

You don't need to know about those weeks and months of soul-searching, how he could not put the loss away, how it was there every time he went to bed and every morning when he woke up, how he thought about changing every single thing about himself. Players called to say how much they loved him. Friends called to help. South Carolina's Eddie Fogler was particularly helpful. Fogler is a blunt man. "Hey, you finished 34-2," Fogler said. "A lot of teams finished 2-34."

He appreciated all of them, but he could not make the loss go away. He could not make it stop hurting. How hard was the loss, Roy? What kind of question is that? There are no words for the pain of losing. There are no words for the despair you feel when you wonder whether there's something missing inside.

The Jayhawks are back. They are playing well. Williams leads the way again. He has shortened practices. People seem to think he is more intense, more angry. That has been written many times, talked about all year. But players say he screams less.

"Definitely less," All-American Raef LaFrentz says.

"I don't think there's any question that coach Williams has been easier on us this year," Ryan Robertson says.

"I think Coach has pulled back a little," All-American Paul Pierce says.

Truth is, Williams is probably not more intense nor less. He's just Roy Williams, same as always, determined as ever, brilliant still. That was the answer he came up with after the Arizona loss. He decided to stay the same.

"The key," Roy Williams says, "is to get stronger and keep going."

*   *   *

Question: "How hard was last year's tournament loss to Arizona, Roy?"

Roy Williams smiles. He looks at the reporter. He touches his gray hair. He twangs his answer.

"It was hard," he says. "But we're not talking about that anymore."

— March 15, 1998

DirecTV: Grounds for Divorce?

Well, the marriage had a nice run. We had 11 wonderful months together. We honeymooned. We visited each other's parents. We went out with other married couples. We bought a nice house on a quiet street. We took up the carpet. We picked out wallpaper. We might have gone on forever.

Except for Rick.

Rick's the DirecTV guy.

Rick put in DirecTV, this satellite system, Friday morning. I thought I could handle it. I handled cable. I hardly watched it at all, except for some baseball and golf and the last couple of minutes of NBA games and hockey and an occasional billiards show on ESPN.

That's all ESPN has anymore is an occasional billiards show.

Yes, it was in moderation. I thought I could handle it. But I've been sitting in this room for seven hours. I have watched highlights from a 1981 Jets-Packers game, and I have seen an old Oscar De La Hoya-Julio Caesar Chavez fight, and I have glimpsed George Plimpton interview Lou Brock, and at night I can choose from seven baseball games, two hockey games, one auto race, four golf instruction shows, two fishing exhibitions, 27 sports quiz shows, and three different showings of the movie "Ronin."

In the morning, I can watch highlights of the 1955 Stanley Cup.

I am never, ever leaving this room again.

This strategy surely will cause some problems because we have not actually moved all of our furniture into the new house, and the in-laws are coming in for the weekend, and wallpaper isn't actually on the walls, and the grass in the front yard is high enough that you half expect ghosts from "Field of Dreams" to come walking out, but I don't care.

I just don't care anymore.

Oooh, look — old guys playing tennis.

Rick warned this could be hypnotic. He warned that, if you're not careful, you will just sit around and watch sports, and life will drift away and, uh, well, he said something or other after that, but I wasn't really paying attention because the Orioles and Mets were playing in the 1969 World Series.

They should offer psychological tests before selling these things. Some people can handle it. They watch sports for a little while and then get bored. My wife, Margo, bless her heart, watched two innings of the Royals game and then switched the television to "Lost In Space." She switches back, from time to time, to check on a score. That's enough for her. That's enough for most normal people.

Not me. Not my family. If DirecTV had been invented 32 years ago, I never would have been born. My father would have been watching a Washington Senators game. Put it this way: My father would watch two kids play Rock 'Em, Sock 'Em Robots on TV if there was a couch nearby.

These days, no joke, my father watches sports in a recliner that has been broken for at least eight years. Technically, it does not even qualify as a chair anymore. It's closer to a garbage bag with metal parts sticking out of it. Pierre Bauchemin, the world's most renowned contortionist, couldn't sit in that chair. My father sits in it for days at a time, watching World Championship Chess, Sumo Skeet Shooting, whatever. He doesn't even know the chair's broken.

I pledged to be different. Sophisticated. Ambitious. A life grabber. Earlier this week I promised Margo that I would take her to the opera. Sure. La Boheme, perhaps.

Then, Rick walked in. Maybe this will pass. Maybe I will grow up. In the meantime, I better go check to see whether Margo has left me yet. Right after the 1992 Hooters 500.

— **May 8, 1999**

CHARLIE BROWN WILL NEVER
BOOT THAT BALL

First, it was Michael Jordan. Then John Elway. Then Barry Sanders. The great ones just keep walking away from us. But none of those departures quite reaches the sadness of this retirement party. The athlete of the century has retired. Forget all the other lists. This athlete graced sports for almost 50 years, and not one sport, no, baseball and football and hockey and tennis and checkers and kite-flying, too. No one can ever replace him.

Then, no one would ever want to replace him.

"Oh," Charlie Brown says to the assembled reporters. "Good grief."

*　　　*　　　*

Charlie Brown almost kicked the football in 1968. Lucy looked up at him and said, "Look at the innocence in my eyes." He trusted her, and he ran to kick the ball, and she pulled it away. He landed on his back.

"What you have learned today," she told him, "will be of immeasurable value to you for many years to come."

*　　　*　　　*

First and foremost, Charlie Brown loved baseball. He dreamed about baseball. One time he dreamed he was on the field, a beautiful spring day, and he wondered what a pitcher's mound would say if it could talk. "Why don't you learn how to pitch, you stupid kid?" the pitcher's mound said.

He lived to pitch. And he lost hundreds and hundreds of games in a row. He got his clothes knocked off by line drives. The losing scores were staggering. Forty-eight to nothing. Seventy-three to nothing. Once, he got to pitch relief for the great Peppermint Patty team of 1981. Peppermint Patty's team led 50-0 with two outs in the ninth when Charlie Brown came in. He gave up 51 runs.

"I left you a 50-run lead!" Peppermint Patty screamed at him over the phone, the very same thing Tony Muser screamed often last year. "How could you blow a 50-run lead?"

"I'm sorry," Charlie Brown said in a disguised voice. "Mr. Brown is not in. If you'd care to leave your number, he'll try to get back to you sometime next year."

But there won't be a next year. Peanuts creator Charles Schulz has colon cancer and is retiring.

*   *   *

Charlie Brown almost kicked the football in 1970. Lucy cried when at first he refused to try. "Wah!" she cried. "You don't trust me. You think I'm no good." He trusted her, and he ran to kick the ball, and she pulled it away. He landed on his back.

"Never," she told him, "listen to a woman's tears."

*   *   *

Managing the baseball team took a lot out of Charlie Brown. He could not sleep before games. "I wonder," he said late one night in 1953 as he gazed out the window, "if Casey Stengel is sleeping."

He tried to be a tough manager. But it wasn't in him. Once, Snoopy fell asleep during a game and dropped a fly ball. Charlie Brown got in Snoopy's face and screamed. Seconds later, he felt terrible. "I'm sorry, Snoopy," he pleaded. "I apologize. I shouldn't have been so sarcastic. I guess I don't know how to handle players. I'm a terrible manager. I apologize."

The next pitch, Snoopy fell asleep, and a fly ball dropped behind him.

What a team. Snoopy slept. Schroeder, his catcher, cared only about his music. Linus would bring his blanket with him to the plate. Pig Pen, at second base, was so dirty he blended into the infield. And there was Lucy, an outfielder who had an ongoing duel with routine fly balls.

"I got it," she screamed during one memorable game. She settled under the ball. The ball dropped in front of her.

" 'I got it' could mean a lot of things," she said.

Until 1993, the team won only one real game. They did win back-to-back forfeits in the late 1960s. The one game they won on the field happened when Charlie Brown, overtaken by nerves because his beloved little red-haired girl was in the stands watching, had to go home. Linus came in and pitched a shutout, earning a victory and a hug from the little red-haired girl.

"My friend!" Charlie Brown wailed.

But he could not be angry with Linus for long. Charlie Brown could never hold a grudge. He always believed that something good would happen. He always hoped.

"Quick, Charlie Brown, go to the front door," Lucy screamed one day. "Ted Williams is there to see you. He wants some advice on how to manage a baseball team."

Charlie Brown ran to the door. No one was there. Suddenly, from behind, he heard Lucy laughing and screaming, "April Fool." Charlie Brown stood on the front porch alone.

"It could have happened," he said.

*   *   *

Charlie Brown almost kicked the football in 1976. Actually Lucy told him: "I'm going to pretend to hold the football, Charlie Brown. But when you come running up to kick it, I'm going to pull it away, OK?" He ran to kick the ball, and she pulled it away. He landed on his back.

"Men never really listen to what women are saying, do they?" she asked.

*   *   *

Charlie Brown's heart belonged to just two people. The little red-haired girl. And that inconceivably mediocre ballplayer, Joe Shlabotnik.

"I remember one game last year," Charlie Brown said, "he came up to bat in the ninth inning and said he was going to hit a home run."

"Did he?" Linus asked.

"No," Charlie replied. "He popped up. But he ran it out."

He wrote often to Joe Shlabotnik but got no reply. He was president of the Joe Shlabotnik fan club. He once offered Lucy a Mickey Mantle baseball card, a Hank Aaron, a Willie Mays, a Whitey Ford, a Sandy Koufax, a Maury Wills and a Joe Garagiola for one Joe Shlabotnik. She said no because she thought he was kind of cute. After he walked away in agony, she threw the Joe Shlabotnik card away. Decided he wasn't that cute after all.

The killer came that day when he spent his life savings to go to a sports banquet, where Charlie Brown would finally meet Joe Shlabotnik. All the stars were there. Snoopy saw his old friend and skating partner Peggy Fleming. Linus saw Jack Nicklaus and Bobby

Orr.

"Joe Shlabotnik, where are you?!" Charlie Brown screamed as the lights went out. The next day they read in the paper that Joe Shlabotnik was the only athlete not to show up.

"Joe apologized to reporters this morning," Linus read out loud. "He explained that he had marked the wrong date on his calendar, the wrong city and the wrong event."

"He's your hero Charlie Brown," Linus said.

*   *   *

Charlie Brown almost kicked the football in 1984. Lucy gave him a contract that she would not pull the ball away. A signed contract! He trusted her, of course, and he ran to kick the ball, and she pulled it away. He landed on his back.

"Now that I look at this contract," Lucy said, "I notice it's not notarized."

*   *   *

His life was more than baseball, though. One year, Charlie Brown coached a football team.

"Will it be a good team?" Lucy asked.

"Well, I'm not sure," Charlie Brown said.

"Vince Lombardi, he ain't," Lucy said.

There was the year that Snoopy decided he wanted to play tennis at Wimbledon but for some strange reason was convinced that Wimbledon was being played in Kansas City.

"Kansas City!" Snoopy screamed. "Wow, what a place." He looked for the ocean. Couldn't find it. Looked for Wimbledon. Couldn't find that either.

"Didn't I tell you Wimbledon isn't near Kansas City?" Charlie Brown asked when Snoopy returned.

"I think they moved it so I wouldn't get to play," Snoopy said.

All around, Charlie's friends played their games. Snoopy became a star hockey goalie ("They do not sleep well in Montreal tonight," Snoopy said). Woodstock, the little bird, worked on his outfield play ("Use two hands," Snoopy yelled after a fly ball squashed Woodstock). Peppermint Patty thought she was chosen by an angel to give the world a message, and the message was "If a foul ball is hit behind third base, it's the shortstop's play." ("I expect to be persecuted," she said).

Lucy kept dropping fly balls ("I think I've got it," she started screaming as she settled under fly balls, because, as she said, the older you get the less sure you are about things).

And all along, Charlie Brown just kept on going, kept on trying to win the baseball game (he finally did hit a game-winning home run in 1993, sending America into an uproar), kept on trying to win over his beloved little red-haired girl, kept on thinking he would meet his hero, Joe Shlabotnik. Now, he retires. Sports will never be the same.

"I saw the most unbelievable football game ever played," Linus said, and he proceeded to tell about how a team had been on its own 1 with 3 seconds to play, and the quarterback had dropped back, and he had thrown to a receiver who whirled around four guys and ran 99 yards. People stormed the field, laughing and screaming, and players rolled around on the ground and danced. It was fantastic.

Charlie Brown looked at him.

"How did the other team feel?" he asked.

*   *   *

Charlie Brown was the first athlete to see a sports psychologist. She was Lucy, of course. And in 1969, he was feeling particularly low. Lucy decided to set him straight.

"You, Charlie Brown, are a foul ball in the line drive of life," she said. "You're in the shadow of your own goal posts.... You are a miscue.... You are three putts on the 18th green.... You are a 7-10 split in the 10th frame.... A love set.... You have dropped a rod and reel in the lake of life.... You are a missed free throw, a shanked 9-iron and a called third strike. Do you understand? Have I made myself clear?"

Charlie Brown looked at her with a blank face.

"Just wait till next year!" he screamed.

Now, there is no next year. Charlie Brown retires. He will never, ever get to kick that football. Good grief, my friends. Good grief indeed.

— Jan. 2, 2000

THE NICEST GUY IN SPORTS

You will not believe a word of this story. You will not believe a word of it because there's no way Mike Sweeney can be real. No way he's this nice. No way he's this All-American. No way he's this wholesome. No way.

Many people believe they would be the nicest guy in pro sports, if given the chance, if given the talent, if given the money. Mike Sweeney actually is the nicest guy in pro sports. He signs every autograph. He speaks at churches. He hugs everybody. He lives the life, nonstop.

He's like a castaway from some fuzzy, cornball, black-and-white baseball movie, you know the kind, where our hero promises to hit a home run for little Jimmy in the hospital. Then our hero goes to the ballpark and wallops a home run. Then little Jimmy miraculously gets out of bed and walks as music plays in the background. And the nurses cry.

That kind of movie.

Mike Sweeney's that kind of baseball hero.

You're not going to believe any of it, not in this day and age, not even on a Fourth of July weekend. Here's a good little implausible story just to start you off. Before the season, Sweeney signed a contract with the Royals for $2.25 million. That's what happens when you drive in 100 runs and score 100 runs in the same season. Yep, $2.25 mil, more money than Sweeney figured to see in his life. Just a few years before, he was a repo man in California, for crying out loud.

So, his New York agents told him to spend a little of the money on something frivolous. Hey, they told him, you waited all your life to hit the jackpot. Go wild. Buy yourself a new car. A boat. Some jewelry. Something.

Sweeney nodded. He understood.

He went out and bought himself a guitar.

Now, every night, he tries to play it and sing songs of worship.

No, you're not going to believe a word of this.

*   *   *

Our story begins in an incubator. Inside was a little, baby Mike Sweeney, born a bit prematurely in southern California. In there with him was a plastic baseball bat. It was placed there lovingly by Mike Sweeney Sr.

"I was hoping," Mike Sr. said, "to influence him a little."

Mike Sweeney Sr. dreamed the baseball dream first. He played in the California Angels' system for a couple of seasons. But shortly before Mike Jr., the first son, was born, the father realized that some dreams just don't come true. He quit baseball and got a job driving a truck for a beer distributor.

When Mike was born, the father put a baseball bat in the incubator.

Yes, this is that kind of corny story.

"Let me tell you how I feel about the guy," Royals manager Tony Muser said. "I have a daughter, OK? Now, I don't want her to marry Michael Sweeney. But I want her to marry someone like Michael Sweeney."

This is how people talk about Mike Sweeney Jr. The man is 6 feet 3 and 225 pounds, built like a freight train. He has banged and chiseled himself into one of the great hitters in baseball. He's among the top five in the American League in a half-million offensive categories, including batting average, batting average with runners in scoring position, batting average against lefties, hits, singles, doubles, sacrifice flies and RBIs. Nobody in the league has been hit by as many pitches, a sure sign of respect.

The man is hitting .714 with the bases loaded.

But, somehow, people don't talk about that when they talk about Mike Sweeney. They talk about, well, the nicest guy in sports.

"When I have children," reads a letter from Spence Shoen of Lenexa, "I will tell them to look up to Mike Sweeney."

"I want to commend Mike Sweeney for the professional but humble way he conducts himself on and off the field," goes a letter from John Hulen in Overland Park.

"Once, a couple of years ago, I went down to talk to him," goes a letter from someone we'll leave unidentified. "I was drunk as a skunk but he stayed and talked and even signed a ball."

Letters like this pour in two or three times a week, year-round. Sweeney gets thousands of letters, thanking him for showing up at someone's birthday party, staying out until 1 a.m. to sign autographs, or spending a half-hour in the grocery store, near the cereal boxes, talking about the role God has played in his life.

There are good people throughout sports, people like Will Shields, who gives so much of his time and love, or Tom Watson, who has raised millions of dollars for Children's Mercy Hospital. Yes, there are many good people.

But nobody is quite as nice as Mike Sweeney.

"There's just something in his eyes," said Richard Sweeney, Mike's brother and best friend. "I don't say that because he's my brother. When you talk to him, you can just tell there's something in his eyes. There's something in his soul. He's always had that, as long as I can remember."

*   *   *

A quick interlude: One game, earlier this year, Mike Sweeney struggled at the plate. He tears himself apart after games like that. He went to the indoor batting cage and ripped line drive after line drive, and he barked at himself between pitches.

"COME ON MIKE!"

"DRIVE THE BALL!"

"COME ON!"

After that, he took his bats into the clubhouse and slammed them down hard in his locker. His face turned red. His eyes burned. When a ballplayer looks like that you learn to avoid him the way you would avoid a growling Doberman.

So we avoided him.

Only, then, he came up to us.

"Hi," he said sheepishly. "How's your wife? How was your Easter?"

*   *   *

Mike Sweeney grew up in a big Irish Catholic family that lived in a house on Tam O' Shanter Lane. From that simple sentence, you can probably imagine the childhood Mike Sweeney lived in Ontario, Calif., just a half-hour from Anaheim. You know the life, church and picnics and mischief and barbecues and sprinklers and broken windows where the baseballs hit.

"I wasn't perfect," Sweeney said, but except for one day when he skipped school and headed for the beach and one wonderful story where he ended up being escorted home by a policeman (more on that one later), everybody around Sweeney remembers him being just that: perfect.

"Except for when that policeman came," Richard Sweeney said, "I can't remember him every doing anything wrong. Ever .... Even when he was a kid, Mike was one of those guys — everyone looked up to him. It's not like in the movies, you know, where everybody loves the party guys. Mike didn't drink or do drugs or party or anything like that. Everybody just admired Mike.

Mike grew up in two places mainly, church on Sunday and Home Run Park batting cage in Anaheim during the week. Mike Sr. gave batting lessons to kids there to make a few extra dollars. Mike Jr. started hitting there when he was 3 years old, in the slowest batting cage. Other kids mark their childhood with pencil marks on a wall. For Mike Jr., childhood meant stepping up from the slowest batting cage to the medium speeds to, finally, the fastest cage.

"He could hit," Mike Sr. says. "That was a gift. When he was 8 or 9, I sat him down and told him he was a pretty good little baseball player. And I said, 'If you like the game, and you play hard, it might pay for your college.' He took that to heart."

From then on, Mike Jr. dreamed of playing big-league baseball. Sure, he had these big, corny suburban dreams. He and his best friend, Greg Thewes, used to sit at the Denny's just around the block from the house and make plans. Big plans. They would go to college together. They would each meet their wives there. They would buy homes next door. They would have cookouts together. Greg would go to the Olympics as a track star. Mike would play major-league baseball. They had it all figured out.

Greg's an accountant in California now.

Mike should be selected to the American League All-Star team.

Of course they still talk just about every week.

*   *   *

A quick interlude: One game, a couple of weeks ago, Mike Sweeney was rounding third, heading for home. The ball arrived first. Now, the one thing about Sweeney that flusters Muser just a bit is that maybe he's a bit too nice. Every game, for instance, Sweeney will chat away with the guy on first base. "MICHAEL!" Muser will scream, though he sometimes calls Sweeney "REVEREND!"

"MICHAEL!" Muser screams. "QUIT TALKING TO THAT GUY ON FIRST BASE!"

Anyway, so Sweeney headed home, and the ball was there first, and let's face it, baseball isn't for nice guys. Baseball is a hard game. Sweeney plowed into Anaheim's Bengie Molina.

"Attaboy!" Muser screamed. "Way to go Michael! Way to go!"

But Sweeney did not hear. Sweeney got up in a heartbeat and rushed over to Molina to make sure he was OK.

*   *   *

Sure, Muser figured Sweeney was too nice to play this game. The kid called him "Sir." He led the team in prayer. He never swore. Ever. Half of baseball is swearing, for pete's sake.

No, this kid wasn't tough enough, Muser felt sure of that. And Muser didn't like the way he caught. And the kid wasn't hitting for power. And he wasn't hitting for average either. And he was too nice. And Muser thought he couldn't call much of a game. And he didn't walk enough. And he was slower then Christmas.

And he was too nice.

But, for some reason, when the Royals talked about trading Sweeney before last season, it was Muser who stepped in and said 'No.' There was something about that kid Sweeney. Maybe it was the fact that he hardly ever struck out. Muser just loved that. Sweeney, even when he wasn't hitting well, had this amazing knack for putting the ball in play. He battled. That was a gift from God and the Home Run Park batting cage and an old high school coach who used to give out a big box of Special K to the man on the team who struck out the most times.

"I didn't want that big box," Sweeney said. "So I didn't strike out."

OK, it was more than just Sweeney's lack of strikeouts. Muser may play the crusty, gruff, harsh old manager, but the guy's got a heart ticking, and he fell for Mike Sweeney just like anybody else. The kid played so hard, he cared so much, he was so gosh-darned polite. Instead of trading Sweeney, Muser walked up to him one day and said: "Michael, I think you're going to be a good hitter in this league. We're going to get you some at-bats and prove it to everybody."

And Sweeney said: "Thank you, sir. I won't let you down."

He actually said that.

Sweeney hit .322 with 22 homers, 102 RBI, 101 runs scored, and he was second in the American League with 44 doubles.

This year, he's hitting even better, much better, and, he's turning himself into a decent first baseman. If New York Yankees manager Joe Torre has a heart ticking inside, he will pick Sweeney for the All-Star Game.

Sweeney would call him "Sir," also.

*　　　*　　　*

A quick interlude: You ask Mike Sweeney about his favorite memory, and he won't talk about the 13 straight games when he had an RBI (an American League record) or his 25-game hitting streak he had last season or some fish he caught on his annual fishing outing or even the time he spent in Germany last year teaching kids baseball and talking about his faith.

No, his favorite memory goes like this: He was 8, and the family had just moved to the new house. It was Christmas Eve. He turned to his Dad and said, "We need a Christmas tree." So, they went out, father and son, for five hours, looking everywhere for a Christmas tree on Christmas Eve.

"What does money mean," Mike Sweeney asked, "compared to that?"

*　　　*　　　*

What you notice about Mike Sweeney as a hitter is he almost

never has a bad at-bat. That's how George Brett was. Sweeney is ferocious every time up (that's what Muser loves about him), he really won't strike out (he has struck out eight times in his last 150 at bats), he won't hit routine fly balls and he won't often hit soft ground balls back to the pitcher.

You want to get him out, you have to earn it.

"When Mike gets into a zone, he hits everything hard," Royals third baseman Joe Randa said. "That's one thing about him. He walks up to the plate and you know he's going to hit the ball hard."

Sure, Sweeney thinks that comes from his life. His faith. Everything comes together. Baseball and faith. Church and the batting cage. He goes to church every Sunday, of course, and he attends numerous Bible studies and he prays every day. You can't go at religion casually. He hits off the tee every day, the most boring thing in sports. You can't hit halfheartedly.

You can't face a pitcher without spirit.

You can't go at life without trying.

The thing is, Sweeney figures, you have to hit the ball hard, you have to live life hard. You have to care about what you're doing all the time. Most athletes, actually, are pretty nice. They usually will sign autographs for free. They often visit hospitals at Christmas. They give of their time generously. Most athletes are pretty darned nice.

The reason they are not quite as nice as Mike Sweeney is that it's hard to be that nice. It's tough to sign autographs until 1 a.m., then go home and read your daily Bible verse every night. It's hard to get in late from a road trip, then wake up early, go teach 300 kids how to hit a baseball, then run across town to run a charity golf tournament, then sign 40 autographs while you're trying to eat dinner.

Even for Mike Sweeney, it's hard to be cheery all the time, every minute, even when you're in a major slump, even when the team's not winning, even when you're missing your brother's wedding, even when you just want to go home and get a little sleep but you can't because the line of people stretches across the parking lot.

Of course it's hard.

The point is you are never supposed to have a bad at-bat.

"People who work hard," it says in Ecclesiastes, "sleep well, whether they eat little or much."

"Mike and I have never talked about this," Mike Sr. says. "But you hear how some athletes say they don't want to be role models. Mike wants to be a role model, I think. That's important to him. He loves people. He loves kids. He wants to inspire people, I think."

*   *   *

OK, you want to hear about the time Mike Sweeney got in trouble with the law. He was 12 years old, and every single week, he and a few friends would wrap toilet paper around the same house. Well, sure enough, one day the owner came running out of the house and caught them Charmin-handed.

Everybody took off, including Sweeney. He hopped on his bicycle and rushed away. He had made it. But all of a sudden, he heard one of his friends behind him, crying. One of his friends had been nabbed. Everyone else had escaped, and Sweeney had escaped too, but he could not help himself.

He went back to help his friend.

That's how he got caught.

The man called the police, and the policeman decided this was a good time to scare these kids straight. You couldn't have toilet paper all over Ontario, for crying out loud. So, he told them they were going to jail, going away for a long time, and before that little speech was over, Sweeney was crying. The policeman took him home in the police car. Sweeney showed up on the doorstep in tears with a policeman.

Even now, Sweeney remembers that day vividly. You could say it was just childish mischief, certainly toilet-papering a house is not a felony offense. But you have to understand: It might just have been the worst thing Mike Sweeney has ever done.

"Crime doesn't pay," Sweeney said, and he laughs, and he smiles at a little boy nearby, and he praises the waitress for fine service, and he goes outside and shakes hands firmly and asks people their names, and he goes out the ballpark and gets three hits, then he signs autographs until way past midnight.

Then he goes home and plays his new guitar and sings to the Lord.

Told you that you wouldn't believe a word of it.

But then, you've got to have a little faith.

HOW TO BE LIKE MIKE

10:00 a.m.: Wake up.

10:30 a.m.: Make an omelet or go to First Watch. Be courteous to waiters and waitresses.

11-2 p.m.: Call friends and family. Read. Pray. Do charitable work, if there's an opportunity.

2:30-3 p.m.: Arrive at the ballpark, read and answer fan mail.

3-6 p.m.: Prepare for game.

6 p.m.: Sign autographs and talk to people.

7:05 p.m.: Play game.

10 p.m. (approximately): Work out after game.

11:15 p.m.: Go out and sign autographs for every person waiting.

Midnight: Head home. Play guitar and sing songs of worship.

1 a.m.: Call friends and family. Read. Maybe watch a DVD.

2:30 a.m.: Read daily Bible verse.

3 a.m.: Go to sleep.

— July 2, 2000

DERRICK THOMAS, 1967-2000

MIAMI — People wander in and out of Jackson Memorial Hospital now, some crying, some laughing, some trying hard to look brave. Newcomers drift through the halls aimlessly. Regulars walk with purpose, like police officers on the beat. A few hours have gone by since Derrick Thomas died so suddenly. Night falls. Rain drizzles. The hospital goes on. The hospital always goes on.

Derrick Thomas was just one man in this gigantic assembly of hospital buildings. Just one story. In the various children's wards at Jackson Memorial — the kinds of places that Derrick so often visited during his life — little kids deal with the most terrible kinds of pain: cancer, leukemia, paralysis, cystic fibrosis. Across a half-dozen halls, across parking lots, people cling to their last days. Babies are born. People die young. Rape victims try to put their lives back together. Doctors massage human hearts, trying to make them pump again.

Yes, in every building, they all have stories.

Derrick Thomas was just one story. He grew up in Miami, an angry kid who never understood exactly why his father did not come home. He would wait for his father all his childhood. Every single day, he used to say, he had this faint feeling that Robert Thomas would just suddenly burst through the door. Even after Derrick had given up all real hope, even when he felt all this wildness running through him and he just had to let it out on the Miami streets, even when everything in his entire body told him that Robert Thomas would never come home, that faint feeling would never quite go away. Derrick Thomas stared at doors.

Air Force Capt. Robert Thomas was some kind of man. He was a brilliant student, a teacher for a short while, and, at last, a hero. He was the last man to eject from a burning plane as it fell over North Vietnam. Derrick Thomas last saw his father when he was 5. When Derrick was 13, his father's body was flown back from Vietnam.

Derrick Thomas held his father's spirit close after that.

And, surely, it was his father's spirit that helped push Derrick Thomas to become the man he became. He played football fiercely. He lived fiercely. He partied hard and read books to children in the library on Saturday mornings. He rushed the quarterback with terrible and wonderful vengeance, and he carried the biggest presents to the sickest little kids at Christmas. He was like a big kid himself so much of the time, smiling huge, mocking everybody around him. He was party coordinator at the Pro Bowl in Hawaii, the guy who yelled loudest at his teammates at halftime, the man who every year predicted he would set the NFL sack record.

He always played his best games closest to Veterans Day, after the jets roared over Arrowhead Stadium.

No, Robert Thomas was never too far away. You always wonder what drives a football player to bear his soul on the field, to fearlessly throw his body into the blur, to play with that kind of unchecked fury. For all those years, Derrick Thomas relentlessly chased after quarterbacks, knocked footballs free and turned around so many games with just one bold play. No matter what anyone thinks, you can't play football like that just for money or fame or ego or the cheers. There has to be something more.

"My father," Derrick Thomas said softly in those rare moments when you could get him to talk softly.

The sadness always strikes a little harder when an athlete dies young. It's hard to say exactly why. Maybe it's because Derrick

Thomas made so many people in Kansas City feel more alive. He made folks jump out of their chairs and scream at the television. He made Sundays a bit brighter. He made children smile. When he was at his best, Derrick Thomas always seemed to move just an instant before anybody else on the field. And it was thrilling. It's hard to imagine he's gone. It's hard to understand.

Jackson Memorial Hospital goes on on a dreary night in Miami. An ambulance siren wails. A worried mother sobs softly in a waiting room. A doctor promises to do the best he can. This is life and death, even for remarkable athletes, even for remarkable men, and the only comfort left is the unmistakable feeling that Robert Thomas sits in heaven now and waits for his oldest son to burst through the door.

— Feb. 9, 2000